THE STATE AND THE POLITICS OF CULTURE

A Critical Analysis of the National E ... *s*

Jerry Henderson

University Press of America,® Inc.
Lanham · Boulder · New York · Toronto · Oxford

Copyright © 2005 by
Jerry Henderson

University Press of America,® Inc.
4501 Forbes Boulevard
Suite 200
Lanham, Maryland 20706
UPA Acquisitions Department (301) 459-3366

PO Box 317
Oxford
OX2 9RU, UK

Library of Congress Control Number: 2005924845
ISBN 0-7618-3180-0 (paperback : alk. ppr.)

⊖™ The paper used in this publication meets the minimum
requirements of American National Standard for Information
Sciences—Permanence of Paper for Printed Library Materials,
ANSI Z39.48—1984

This book is dedicated to the artists—past and present—for understanding the importance and relationships of artistic expressions in the development of social, spiritual, political, and economic culture and values.

Contents

Tables

Figures

Preface

The State and the Politics of Culture: A Critical Analysis of the National Endowment for the Arts was first submitted as a proposed thesis topic to the faculty of Atlanta University's Department of Political Science (Atlanta, Georgia) in partial fulfillment of the requirement for the degree of Master of Arts. The book adds another rare opportunity to view arts in relationship to politics and government. In 1939, Grace Overmyer's book, *Government and the Arts*, raised significant issues relative to this subject. Four decades later, Milton C. Cummings, Jr., of Johns Hopkins University Department of Political Science (Baltimore, Maryland), offered another look at government and the arts in *Government and the Arts in Europe, North America, and Japan* and with J. Mark Davidson Schuster (Ed.) *Who's to Pay for the Arts? The International Search for Models of Arts Support.* More recently, David Caute has added to the body of literature with *The Dancer Defects: The Struggle for Cultural Supremacy During the Cold War.* Because of the importance of the arts and the role of government, there is a need for more research and analysis, especially by the academic community.

The proposal was submitted to Atlanta University in the 1980s and was presented as a descriptive and theoretical research effort that would constitute a critical examination of the National Endowment for the Arts (NEA). In an attempt to discern to what extent the Endowment had or had not realized its stated objectives, the author collected data and analyzed the organization's stated objectives, its values, programs, and its grant allocation and staffing procedures. The work specifically focused on certain institutions and organizations, both cultural and educational, that receive substantial support from the Endowment.

The theoretical assumption of the research effort rests on the premise that the federal government, by way of the National Endowment for the Arts, plays a vital role in maintaining cultural hegemony of a particular race and class. The book advances two general hypothesis: (1) the interwoven bureaucracy of the NEA is structured in a way that prevents maximum participation in its programs by the broader arts community, and (2) black and smaller cultural/educational institutions and organizations receive minimum support from the Endowment.

Chapter One traces the evolutionary process of the Endowment's creation. It also looks at the principal laws that were instrumental in its establishment and on its bureaucratic structure. Chapter Two looks at activities that were designed to increase support to the Endowment and proposed legislation to increase support. The role of the government (particular in President Jimmy Carter's administration) is closely examined. Chapter Three examines the NEA in terms of its ability to execute its programs and categorize applications and discusses the review process, decision-making, and staffing procedures. Chapter Four focuses on the "politics of the Endowment" and its relationship to maintaining cultural values in American society.

Acknowledgments

I graciously acknowledge three of my former professors in particular: Dr. Mack H. Jones (my thesis advisor), Dr. Larry Nobles, Jr., and Dr. William Boone. Dr. Jones, Professor of Theory and Methodology and International Relations, was instrumental in this research effort. He provided "academic space," guidance, critiques, feedback, and support. Dr. Nobles, Professor of Constitutional Law, encouraged me to continue this research to the doctoral level, a challenge that interested me but that I eventually left to someone else. Throughout my graduate studies, postgraduate studies, and the many career adventures and experiences since Atlanta University, Dr. Boone, Chairman of the Department of Political Science, has been a continuing academic and professional advisor, as well as a close personal friend.

The questions, comments, suggestions, and criticisms by members and fellow students within the department helped to shape this research. I am indeed most thankful for the support, challenges, and constructive criticism.

I offer a collective acknowledgement to my academic advisor, faculty members, and fellow students. In some way, they all contributed to the writing and direction of this research. They helped to make this book what it is today.

Because of various artistic and cultural associations and relationships, particularly in New York City and Atlanta, Georgia, a number of artists, cultural institutions, and organizations influenced my thinking and encouraged my involvement and active participation in the grassroots arts movement, and no doubt, this particular focus. For this, I offer my humble recognition and salute to the following individuals and organizations: Damani Richard Henderson (my brother, who got me involved), an accomplished actor for two decades, playwright, and director with the nationally acclaimed, award-winning Black Spectrum Theatre Company; Romare Bearden; John O. Killens;

Rube Dee and Ossie Davis; Nikki Giovanni; Maya Angelou; Sonja Sanchez; Hoyt Fuller; Gwendolyn Brooks; Toni Cade Bambari; Judith Jemison; Spike Lee; Amiri Baraka; Jitu Weusi (The East); Andi Gill (New Muse Museum and Cultural Center); Ebon Dooley (Neighborhood Arts Center), Yusef Iman; Alice Lovelace; Osker Spicer; Melanie Rawls (Southern Collective of African-American Writers, SCAAW); Carl Clay and Wayne Garfield, (Black Spectrum Theatre Compay); Kalamu Ya Salaam (*Black Collegiate Magazine*); Dr. Barbara Deen Jackson (New York Metropolitan Museum); Dr. Gerald Deas; Tom Lloyd (StoreFront Museum/Paul Robeson Theatre); Haki Madhubuti (The Institute for Positive Education); John "Watusi" Branch (Afrikan Poetry Theatre); Langston Hughes Library and Cultural Centre; The Last Poets; The Spirit House Movers; The International African Arts and Cultural Festival; The Shrine of the Black Madonna; Woody King, Jr., Jomandi Productions; and many more.

Introduction

I do not believe that it is a necessary effort of a democratic social condition and of democratic institutions to diminish the number of those who cultivate the fine arts, but these causes exert a powerful influence on the manner in which these arts are cultivated. Many of those who have already contracted a taste for the fine arts are impoverished. . . . The number of consumers increases, but opulent and fastidious consumers become scarce. . . . The production of artists are more numerous, but the merit of each production is diminished. . . . In aristocracies, a few great pictures are produced; in democratic countries, a vast number of insignificant ones.

—Alexis de Tocqueville,
Democracy in America

This topic, the *State and the Politics of Culture: A Critical Analysis of the National Endowment for the Arts*, was initially introduced as a proposal into an academic and political environment at Atlanta University (Atlanta, Georgia), Department of Political Science. At the time, the subject did not fit into the category or scope of standard proposals for academic consideration at one of the most politically active political science departments in the United States. This challenge was hurdle number one. I first presented the proposal, as with all other proposals, to my thesis advisor. This was hurdle number two.

After clearing the first and second hurdles, hurdle number three stared me in the face. As dictated by standard procedure and practice, I then presented the proposal to the entire faculty and student body of the department. Their response was to point out serious academic challenges, which I acknowledged and addressed.

The challenges were in part academic, part philosophical, and in part quests for knowledge and better understanding. The research was guided by high academic standards that had been established and maintained over the years by Atlanta University's Department of Political Science. The starting point was to review the literature and trace the history of government's involvement in the arts.

This took me to Grace Overmyer's book, *Government and the Arts*, which focused on "the history, plan of organization, financing and . . . operation of systems used in various countries for the official encouragement and support of the fine arts."[1] Although the book was written years before the establishment of the National Endowment for the Arts, it raised significant concerns then that indeed would pertain to the Endowment.

In her study, which covered some fifty countries, Overmyer pointed out that generally individuals have raised objections to state patronage of the arts. In a chapter titled, "Government Interference with Art?", she indicated that there are basically three reasons for such objections:

(1) That government aid to art, particularly if it included establishment of personal subsidies, serves to foster mediocrity by providing a living for those whose limited talents would cause them, unassisted, properly to abandon the struggle;

(2) That art administrations authorized by government have it in their power to set up standards in accordance with their personal tastes and methods, or with those of some particular school, and thus to discourage production by artists of other tastes and techniques, or to compel their conformance; and

(3) That state assistance may involve official censorship and may promote propaganda.[2]

Overmyer added that the most obvious avenue to censorship in the arts is provided by the stage. She discussed the situation involving the Federal Theatre in which federal government interference was quite evident:[3] "That was in the case of the living newspaper *Ethiopia*, which Washington ordered withdrawn before its opening, on the ground that its subject matter was adversely critical of a foreign power."[4] Overmyer also indicated that there were a "few cases of local interference with Federal Theatre Productions,"[5] and suggested that part of the problems of the Federal Theatre came about as a result of another of its plays, which was titled, "Triple A Plowed Under." She pointed out that this production was "openly critical, not only of the government's farm policies but also of certain of its . . . labor policies; it even went so far as to suggest formation of a new anti-administration political party."[6] Underlying themes from Overmyer's book allude to what C. Wright Mills characterized as "The Cultural Apparatus." In *Power, Politics and People*, Mills maintained that the cultural apparatus is

> . . . composed of all the organizations and milieux in which artistic, intellectual, and scientific work goes on, and of the means by which such work is made available to circles, publics, and masses . . . . It contains an elaborate set of institutions: of schools, laboratories, museums, little magazines, radio networks.[7]

Mills pointed out that "it is in terms of some such conceptions as this apparatus that 'the politics of culture' may be understood."[8] Mills went further than those who merely objected to the role of the state in the administration of the arts. He focused on the entire apparatus as it is constituted. He maintained that

> The prestige of culture is among the major means by which powers of decision are made to seem part of an unchallengeable authority. That is why the cultural apparatus, no matter how internally free, tends in every nation to become a close adjunct of national authority and leading agency of nationalist propaganda.[9]

The movement to establish a national office for the arts in the United States was evolving when Overmyer and Mills were writing about the state and the arts. Their assertions and the arts structures that would evolve began to crystallize at certain points. Mills, in his depiction of the relationship between the establishment and support of the arts and how it impacts the society, wrote that "The money and the public for culture are . . . related. The source and amount of the money, and the extent and nature of the public go far to determine the character of a cultural apparatus."[10] Mills, in giving a historical development of this dimension, wrote that there are basically three stages into which a "natural history of modern culture" tends to fall:

(1) In Europe, including Russia, the modern cultural apparatus begins as a patronage system: Patrons personally support culture and also form the public for which it is produced. The Cultural Apparatus is established upon a precapitalist basis, in close relation to princely house, to church, to monarch, and later to bourgeois patrician. By his work, the cultural workman brings prestige to such higher circles and to the institutions over which they rule. Part of the coterie of these authorities, his status is often ambiguous and insecure: he is usually dependent

upon the whims of The Great Ones, whom he advises, amuses, instructs.

(2)   Then emerges the bourgeois public: The cultural workman becomes an entrepreneur. He earns money by the sale of cultural commodities to anonymous publics. For a brief liberal period in Western history, he stands on common ground with the bourgeois entrepreneur. Both fight against the remnants of feudal control—the businessman to break the bonds of the chartered enterprise, the writer to free himself from the insecurities of patronage. Both fight for a new kind of freedom, for wool and shoes, for an anonymous public for novels and portraits.

(3)   In the Third Stage, which we now enter, several tendencies evident in the Second are carried to their logical outcome: The Cultural Apparatus is established politically or commercially; the cultural workman becomes a man who is qualified, politically or commercially. Both money and public are "provided, and in due course, so are cultural products themselves: Cultural work is not only guided: cultured is produced and distributed—and even consumed—to order. Commercial agencies or political authorities support culture, but unlike older patrons, they do not form its sole public. The public for culture is enormously enlarged and intensively cultivated into the condition of a receptive mass."[11]

Mills concluded that "Today . . . all three stages exist side by side, in one nation or another, in one division of culture or another. Accordingly, the politics of culture and the culture of politics around the world are quite various."[12]

Various divisions and relationships in culture and politics within the United States, in many respects, can be viewed through the role of the National Endowment for the Arts. To help clarify the NEA's complex bureaucracy, this book focuses on its size, structure, racial and ethnic composition, and philosophy. The text analyzes the political and economic status of the Endowment's primary grant recipients. I further present an assessment of the roles of individual panelists and consultants who have been instrumental in the decision-making process of the Endowment. I have attempted to examine carefully the categories of classification as well as descriptions of funding categories. A key aspect of the Endowment is its personnel: Who are they? How are they chosen?

I have further emphasized ethnic and cultural pluralism, as advocated by the Endowment, including distinctions made between the races, policies for affirmative action, and how proposals are awarded and rejected. Issues involving the circumstances under which the

Endowment was established are examined, as well as the laws, rules and regulations that govern its operation.

This research effort examines the Endowment's support to African American cultural institutions and organizations. The information presented reflects the evolution of the Endowment through 1980. The year 1980 met both the academic time frame as well as my personal timeline, which was set for the completion of this research.

Is more research needed on this subject? The answer is *yes*. A comprehensive follow-up and assessment of the National Endowment for the Arts (1980–2000) should be done. I am optimistic that it will be done. Furthermore, I am equally optimistic that this book, as well as books by Overmyer, Cummings[13] and David Caute[14] help to add a wealth of knowledge to the body of literature on this subject.

Notes

1. Grace Overmyer, *Government and the Arts* (New York: W. W. Norton and Company, Inc., 1939), p. 15. Grace Overmyer emphasized the role of the government in the protection and development of the arts. She pointed out that the book was not written to justify or to condemn state aid to the art as an institution. She wrote that "its chief objective has been the assembling of such facts as must form the basis of a just or useful judgment" (p. 10).

2. *Ibid.*, 208.

3. The Federal Theatre was part of President Roosevelt's "New Deal" program under the Works Progress Administration (WPA) to put artists to work. The Federal Writers Project and the Federal Art Project were under this same program. However, the program was destroyed by the Martin Dies Committee.

4. *Ibid.*, 212.

5. *Ibid.*

6. *Ibid.* Also see Bensman, Joseph and Bernard Rosenberg, *Mass, Class and Bureaucracy* (Englewood Cliffs, NJ: Prentice-Hall, Inc., 1963). They concluded by pointing out that in mass culture, "Art is subsidiary: It is an instrumentality." Often it is used as "an inspirational device for stressing patriotism, reinforcing national unity, and heightening morale" (p. 343). Writing on the subject "The Role of the Artist in the Production of Mass Culture," they concluded that "The mass artist may be a talented script writer, a gifted copywriter, or musician. He works for a salary, fee, or commission. He is given an assignment, the substance, outline, and limits of which are prescribed for him. He must obey particular caveats, taboos, and rules of style along lines laid down for him by non-artistic administrators within his organization, or an agency that hires his organization. His work is subject to arbitrary review, revision, and evisceration whenever it fails to meet standards set for him by

higher officials. If his role is important, he must live a respectable, or at least a noncontroversial public life, in accordance with the tenets of respectability defined by mass culture. He should be cooperative and tractable, and free of stubborn streaks and recalcitrance, especially about the nature of his art." (p. 367).

7. C. Wright Mills, *Power, Politics and People: The Collected Essays of C. Wright Mills*, edited by Irving Louis Horowitz (New York: Oxford University Press, 1974), 406.

8. *Ibid.*, 407.

9. *Ibid.*, 410.

10. *Ibid.*, 411.

11. *Ibid.*, 411–412.

12. *Ibid.*, 413.

13. In 1989, Cummings, Jr., offered another book on this subject, *The Patron State: Government and the Arts in Europe, North America, and Japan.* Later, he addressed financing and support for the art in *Who's to Pay for the Arts?: The International Search for Models of Arts Support.*

14. David Caute's *The Dancer Defects: The Cultural Supremacy During the Cold War* discusses how the U.S. and Russia "used the arts as a powerful weapon during the Cold War."

Chapter 1

The National Endowment for the Arts

History

The National Endowment for the Arts is an agency of the federal government that carries out programs of grants-in-aid to arts agencies of the U.S. jurisdiction, to nonprofit, tax exempt organizations, and to individuals of exceptional talent.

The move to establish an official arts agency in the United States can be said to have begun almost two centuries ago. Without any direct mention, the notion of such an agency has prevailed since that time. In 1782, John Adams, second President of the United States stated,

> [I] must study politics and war, that my sons may have liberty to study mathematics and philosophy, geography, natural history and naval architecture, navigation, commerce, and agriculture, in order to give their children a right to study painting, poetry, music, architecture.[1]

George Washington, in an acknowledgement in 1788, declared, "Arts and science are essential to the prosperity of the state and to the ornament and happiness of human life."[2] In 1826, the president of the American Academy of Arts, echoing the same sentiments of the two U.S. presidents, presented a proposal to President John Quincy Adams that suggested that the national government engage in permanent support of the fine arts.[3] In 1859, President James Buchanan formed a National Arts Commission. In 1896, the Public Art League of the United States was organized for the specific purpose of influencing art legislation in Congress. A few years later, in 1910, President William Taft signed a bill creating the Fine Arts Commission, which was to advise the president and Congress on matters relating primarily to the architectural appearance of Washington, D.C.[4]

In 1934, President Franklin D. Roosevelt established the Section of Painting and Sculpture in the Treasury Department as the first official unit of government devoted to decorating post offices and courthouses in the United States. In 1935, President Roosevelt's New Deal Program of the Works Progress Administration (WPA) was expanded to include artists. A number of arts programs were developed. Some estimates indicate that as a result of the New Deal Program, the nation gained more than 2500 murals, 17,000 sculptures, and 108,000 canvasses.[5] During the Seventy-fifth Congress (1937–1938), Washington Congressman John M. Coffee and Florida Senator Claude Pepper presented a fine arts bill to Congress. The Coffee-Pepper bill proposed the establishment of a formal recognition of the arts with the creation of a new bureau. Also in 1937, New York Congressman William I. Sirovich introduced the Federal Arts Act, which contained provisions for a fine arts bureau in the Department of the Interior. It was these and many other endeavors that perhaps inspired President Dwight D. Eisenhower to state in his 1958 State of the Union address that "The Federal Government should give official recognition of the importance of the arts and other cultural activities." It was then up to President John F. Kennedy, who succeeded Eisenhower, to push forward the drive to establish an official arts agency.[6]

In 1962, President Kennedy appointed August Heckscher to the position of Special Consultant on the Arts. In doing so, he directed him to survey and evaluate the impact of existing government programs and policies affecting the arts and make recommendations for future action. On 28 May 1963, Heckscher submitted a report, "The Arts and the National Government," to President Kennedy. The report made three significant recommendations: (1) That the post of Special Consultant on the Arts be made permanent, with its rank raised to that of Special Advisor; (2) That the president establish an Advisory Council on the Arts; and (3) That legislation already pending in Congress to create a National Foundation on the Arts be endorsed. On the recommendations of the report, the President issued an Executive Order that established the Advisory Council on the Arts. When President Lyndon Johnson assumed office following the assassination of President Kennedy, he appointed Roger L. Stevens[7] to the position of Special Assistant to the President on the Arts and gave him the assignment of developing congressional support for a permanent arts agency within the federal government.

In 1964, Congress established the National Council on the Arts to make recommendations on matters relating to the cultural development of the nation.[8] One year later, Congress took the necessary action and created the National Endowment for the Arts. In establishing the Endowment,

> Congress found and declared that the encouragement and support of national progress . . . in the arts, while primarily a matter of private and local initiative, is also a matter of concern to the Federal Government.[9]

On 29 September 1965, President Johnson signed the Arts and Humanities Act, which provided for the creation of the National Endowment for the Arts, with its advisory council, the National Council on the Arts.[10] On 3 September 1969, President Richard Nixon nominated Nancy Hanks[11] as Chairman of the Endowment. After confirmation, she was sworn into office on 6 October 1969.

The Endowment's budget (i.e., total funds for programs) increased from $2,500,000 (1965) to $154,400,000 (1980).[12] It was projected that by mid-1980s, the Endowment's budget would reach $500–600 million.[13] The Endowment's grant funds are appropriated by Congress under three separate classifications:

(1) Program Funds: This money is available to the Endowment to award grants to artists and organizations (including state and regional arts agencies) located throughout the country. Funds are generally awarded for fellowships and various types of projects;

(2) Treasury Funds: This money only becomes available when private donations are received by the Endowment, at which time a special fund matches pledges from outside donors to specific institutions and organizations; and

(3) Challenge Grant Funds: The Challenge Grant Program was established by Congress in 1976. Organizations that receive Challenge Grants must match every federal dollar with at least three dollars from other sources. Grants are awarded on a one-time-only basis but may be spread over three years.[14]

Organizational Design

Table 1 presents the key staff positions and members of the Federal Council. Table 2 presents a history of NEA appropriations from 1966 to 1980. Figure 1 at the end of the chapter illustrates the key positions of the NEA's structure.

Table 1. Members of the Federal Council on the Arts and the Humanities (1978–1979)

Joseph D. Duffy, Chairman, Federal Council on the Arts and the Humanities, and Chairman, National Endowment for the Humanities

Livingston L Biddle, Chairman, National Endowment for the Arts

Ernest L. Boyer, Commissioner, U.S. Office of Education

J. Carter Brown, Chairman, Commission of Fine Arts, and Director, National Gallery of Art

Daniel J. Boorstin, Librarian of Congress, Library of Congress

James B. Rhoads, Archivist of the United States, National Archives and Records Service

Dennis J. Keilman, Acting Commissioner, Public Buildings Service, General Services Administration

William G. Whalem, Director, National Park Service, Department of the Interior

Richard C. Atkinson, Director, National Science Foundation

J. S. Kimmitt, Secretary of the Senate, Executive Secretary of the Senate, Commission on Arts and Antiquities

S. Dillon Ripley, Secretary, Smithsonian Institution

John Reinhardt, Director, International Communication Agency

Fortney H. Stark, Jr., Member, U.S. House of Representatives

Juanita M. Kreps, Secretary, Department of Commerce

Brock Adams, Secretary, Department of Transportation

George C. Seybolt, Chairman, National Museum Service Board

Table 1, Cont'd.

Leila Kimche, Director, Institute of Museum Service
Patricia R. Harris, Secretary, Department of Housing and Urban Development
Paul E. Goulding, Acting Administrator, General Services Administration

Table 2. NEA History of Appropriations (1966–1980)*

Year	Amount $
1966	2,543,308
1967	7,965,692
1968	7,174, 291
1969	7,756,875
1970	8,250,000
1971	15,090,000
1972	29,750,000
1973	38,200,000
1974	60,775,000
1975	74,750,000
1976	82,000,000
1976++	33,937,000
1977	94,000,000
1978	114,000,000
1979	139,660,000
1980=	154,400,000

* See National Endowment for the Arts, *Annual Report*, 1978, pp. 269–271.
++ Appropriations for "Transition Quarter," 1 July 1976 to 30 September 1976.
Fiscal year for U.S. Government changed from 1 July to 1 October.
= See *Chronicle of Higher Education*, "Bill Enacted," 11 February 1980, p. 16.

Staff

The staff of the NEA is spread out to cover, at least in principle, the enormous number of activities and programs that it administers. At the top of Endowments' pyramid is the Office of the Chairman (and staff). Next there are three assistant chairpersons: (1) Assistant to the Chairman/Press, (2) Assistant to the Chairman/Minority Affairs, and (3) Assistant to the Chairman. These positions are followed by the General Counsel for the Arts, the Congressional Liaison Director, the Deputy Chairman for Policy and Planning, and the Director of Policy Development. The program areas are Architecture and Environment

Arts (with a director, assistant director, and staff); Federal Design Unit (staff); Federal Graphics Unit (staff); Dance (director and staff); Education (director and staff); Expansion Arts (director, assistant director, and staff); Music (director, assistant director, and staff); Special Projects, which has a number of components (e.g., Director of Special Projects and Staff; Folk Arts Program, director and staff; Challenge Grants, coordinator and staff); Special Constituencies (coordinator); Theatre (director and staff); Visual Arts, which also has a number of components (director, assistant director, and staff); Craft Coordinator, and Works of Art in Public Places Coordinator; Office of the Budget (director and staff); Evaluation (director and staff); and Grants, which is a very weeded-out component. Within this unit, there are five subdivisions: (1) Grants Officer, Special Assistant to the Grants Officer, and staff; (2) Application Section and staff; (3) Grants Section and staff; (4) Reports/Review Section and staff; and (5) Correspondence Section Supervisor and staff. There is a Program Information Director and staff; *The Cultural Post*, which is the Endowment's newsletter, and its staff; Design Staff; Library and staff; Research (director and staff); Council and Panel Operations (director and staff); and the Office of Secretary to the National Council on the Arts.

In 1979, the staff of the Endowment constituted a total of 324 individuals. These individuals administer the functions of the Endowment. It is in and through these offices and individuals that the bulk of the Endowment's processing activities takes place. At various points within each of the above components, vital decisions are made that help determine who gets what, and why, from the Endowment.

Programs

The Endowment awards grants through eight programs that represent specific arts disciplines: Architecture, Planning, and Design; Dance; Literature; Media Arts; Film/Radio/Television; Museums; Theatre; and Visual Arts; and five interdisciplinary programs: Education, Expansion Arts; Federal-State Partnership; Folk Arts; and Special Projects.

Architecture, Planning, and Design

The Architecture, Planning, and Design Program promotes excellence in design by funding activities in architecture; landscape architecture; urban design; city and regional planning; and graphic, interior, industrial, and other professional design fields. The Architecture, Planning, and Design Program awards grants under two categories: Individuals (e.g., Professional Fellowships), and Organization (e.g., Livable Cities, Design: Communication and Research; and Cultural Facilities Research and Design).

Dance

The Dance Program aids the creative individual, strengthens professional dance companies, makes high quality dance available to new audiences, and encourages the development of new ideas, forms, and techniques. The Dance Program awards grants under three categories: Touring (e.g., Small Company Touring Program, Large Company Touring Program, and Long-Term Dance Engagements), Individuals (e.g., Choreography Fellowships, Film and Video Grants), Dance Organizations (e.g., Choreography, Professional Companies in Residence, Rehearsal Support, Artistic Personnel, and Management and Administration), and Other Organizations (e.g., Dance/Film/Video, and Sponsors of Local Companies).

Education

The chief goal of the Education Program has been to give students and teachers an opportunity to develop an appreciation of art by working with professional artists in the classroom or in community projects. The Education Program awards grants in three categories[15]: Learning Through the Arts; Artist-in-Schools Program; and Arts Administration.

Expansion Arts

The Expansion Arts Program reflects the Endowment's desire to expand the involvement of all Americans in the arts and to encourage the artistic expression of the nation's diverse cultural groups. It carries out these goals by supporting neighborhood and community arts organizations, directed by professionals, in cities, towns, and rural areas. The Expansion Arts Program awards grants in eight categories: Instruction and Training; Arts Exposure Programs; Special Summer Projects; Community Cultural Centers; Services to Neighborhood Arts Organizations; Regional Tour Events; Neighborhoods Arts Consortia; and Comprehensive Technical Assistance Program (a service program).

Federal-State Partnership

The Federal-State Partnership provides basic support for the arts nationwide, as well as grants based on NEA approval of plans. Instead of funding individual artists or arts organizations within a particular discipline, the program administers federal support for the arts through state and regional arts agencies. The Endowment is required by law to make available twenty percent of its program funds appropriated by Congress to these state and regional agencies. The Federal-State Partnership awards grants in three ways: State Grants; Regional Grants; and Grants for Support Services.

Folk Arts

The Folk Arts Program encourages and preserves the traditional arts that are identified with the many subgroups in the nation; these groups share the same ethnic heritage, language, occupation, religion, or geographic area. Among these folk arts are music, dance, song, poetry, tales, oratory, crafts, and rituals. Grants are awarded to such groups as community and cultural organizations, tribes, media centers, educational institutions, professional societies, and state and local agencies. The Folk Arts Program does not have funding categories as such. It supports activities under three broad classifications: presentation of traditional arts and artists, documentation of traditional arts, and inventive and imaginative proposals.

Literature

The Literature Program aids creative writers, including poets, novelists, short story writers, playwrights, essayists, and literary critics. It does so through direct fellowships, funding of residencies for writers, and support for noncommercial magazines and small presses that publish the work of creative writers. The Literature Program awards two types of grants: Individual (e.g., Fellowship for Creative Writers, and Residencies for Writers), and Organizations (e.g., Assistance to Small Presses, and Assistance to Small Presses, and Assistance to Literary Magazines).

Media Arts: Film/Radio/Television

The Media Arts Program helps individuals and organizations produce, exhibit, and preserve film, video, and radio works. The program supports the activities of the American Film Institute in archival work, education, advance training, filmmaker grants, and research and publication. The Media Arts Program also jointly funds projects with the Corporation for Public Broadcasting. With the cooperation of theatre owners, the NEA encourages the showing of what it considers outstanding short films by American filmmakers. The Media Arts: Film/Radio/Television Program awards grants in two basic categories: Organization (e.g., Media Arts Centers, Aid to Film/Video Exhibitions, In-Residence/Workshop Program; Production, and American Film Institute/Arts Endowment Film), and Individuals (e.g., Fellowships, American Film Institute Independent Filmmakers, Video Artists Fellowship, and The Independent Documentary Fund for Public Television).

Museums

The Museum Program offers support for essential museum functions: acquisition, interpretation, and preservation. Art history, science, and children's museums are eligible for grants. Grants are awarded on the merits of the proposed project, location, or operating budget of the museum. The Museum Program awards grants in two categories: Museums and Other Organizations (e.g., Museum Purchase Plan; Special Exhibition; Wider-availability Museums; Cooperative Programs; Utilization of Museum Collections; Catalogue; Conservation; Renovation; Museum Training; and Visiting Specialists) and Individuals (e.g., Fellowships for Museum Professionals).

Music

The goals of the Music Program are to support creativity and excellence in music performance, and to develop informed audiences for music. Grants are awarded to a range of organizations and individuals. The Music Program awards grants in four categories: Orchestras; Ensembles: Contemporary Music; Jazz (e.g., Fellowships for Composer/Performers; Study Fellowships; and Organizations); and Composer/Librettist Fellowship.

Special Projects

Special Projects funds prototype projects that cut across several arts disciplines that are not eligible for funding under any other NEA program and that have potential national or regional impact. The

Special Projects Program awards grants in three categories: Special Projects Category, Grant Program for Arts Centers and Festivals, and Services to the Field.

Theater

The Theater Program primarily aids nonprofit professional theaters. Support goes to companies that present the traditional classics of drama, as well as to those that specialize in new and experimental works. The objectives of the theater programs are threefold: (1) strengthen existing theaters, (2) make high quality theater available to as many Americans as possible; and (3) encourage the development of new talent in the field. The Theater Program awards grants in six categories: Large Professional Theater Companies; Professional Theater Companies with Short Seasons; Small Professional Theater Companies; Professional Theater for Youth; Professional Theater Training; and Professional Theater Touring (Pilot).

Visual Arts

The Visual Arts Program awards fellowships to visual artists working in a wide range of media, and makes grants to nonprofit, tax-exempt organizations to assist visual artists. Grants are awarded in nine categories: Artists' Fellowship; Artists' Spaces; Art in Public Places; Residencies for Artists, Craftsman, Photographers, and Critics; Photography Exhibition Aid; Photography Publications; Photography Surveys; Crafts Exhibition Aid; and Crafts Workshop.[16]

The Endowment has a panel for each of these particular programs:

> In its work, the NEA and the National Council on the Arts are assisted by advisory panels—recognized as knowledgeable individuals who serve the individual programs. Depending on the characteristics of the particular program (i.e., field), this panel may vary. However, they are generally composed of art administrators, artists, board members, and other individuals from a vast range.
>
> More than 500 private citizens serve on these panels. They are appointed by the Chairman (generally three- or four-year terms) with the advice of Council and staff, as well as other organizations and leaders in the field.
>
> Panelists review grants applications, evaluate past programs, and advise Endowment staff and the national Council on the Arts, which is responsible for final recommendations to the Chairman.[17]

This panel system has come under sharp criticism from a House Appropriations Committee Report. The report pointed out that "the panel system or 'peer review system' is the heart of the national Endowment's operations."[18] In this regard, it concluded that the selection of panelists and the panel operation process is the keystone of the Endowment. The report argued that

> The problem in peer review faced by the Endowment is the selection of a panel of experts in a field who can offer quality judgments acceptable to the field because of recognized competence and yet seek an ever-broadening geographical and social representation of the various art disciplines that have traditionally been compartmentalized, specialized, and representative of white Western-European Culture.[19]

Although the investigators acknowledged the fact that most of the individuals are widely recognized and respected in their fields, they argued that the continued reliance by NEA on these individuals creates a "closed circle" of opinion consistently sought and offered to the NEA.[20] The investigators pointed out that

> It was not uncommon for one individual to be chairman of a state's art agency, a member of an NEA program panel, a contract employee of the NEA, and an advisor to other Endowment functions simultaneously. Another NEA panel chairman was a panel member in a different program and under contract to NEA at the same time to perform other functions. In both cases, the individuals were not precluded from other NEA participation, such as receipt of grant funds to affiliated groups, organizations, or the person individually.[21]

In May of 1978, the *Washington International Arts Letter* published a comprehensive listing of panelists and consultants for the Endowment:

> This publication of this list is another first for the *Letter*. Never before under one consolidation could constituents obtain names and addresses of all panelists and consultants to the National Endowment for the Arts. For some years after the Endowment came into being it refused to make known the names of "outside" advisors; then under pressure mainly brought about by this publication it was told to do so by the Senate. Even after that some program directors tried to circumvent the Senate directive.[22]

The *Letter* commented on the credibility of the panelists and consultants by stating that "It has been said that some are known only to their mothers and a few professionals in their fields."[23]

A private foundation consultant charged that "it was possible to lobby personally at the Endowment and find a friend on the panel who can call special attention to a grant request."[24] These and other charges prompted Chairman Biddle to respond by saying that the Endowment had "made special efforts over the past months to examine the panel system and make it more responsive than it was before."[25] The *Washington International Arts Letter* stated,

> Even with recent emphasis on broadening representation, the Investigative Staff found the NEA to rely heavily on what could be termed a "closed circle" of advisors. . . . The composition of task forces, committees, consultants, contractors, and panels represents a repetitive use of the same individuals.[26]

Concerns have also been raised about a number of former staff members of the Endowment who are now employed by Endowment grantees. House Appropriations Chairman Sidney Yates raised this concern with Chairman Biddle. Mr. Biddle responded to Mr. Yates by pointing out, "It was in part a 'compassionate' action and that these people so placed were resources which the world of the arts could not well afford to lose."[27] At this point Yates reminded Biddle of the policies and criticisms that had been focused on former employees of the Defense Department and jobs obtained with contractors in the military-industrial complex. Biddle did not reply to these comments raised by Congressman Yates.[28]

Many of the charges against the Endowment were not new. In 1977, when the Endowment received its largest appropriations up until that time ($96 million), Representative Yates complained that "the arts agency financed only established groups."[29]

In response to much of the criticism that had been raised from various concerns, in August of 1978, for the first time in its history, the Endowment adopted a statement of policy. Its goals and policies were stated in its Preamble, which read,

> This statement of goal of the National Endowment for the Arts, its role and responsibilities in the artistic life of the nation, is rooted in certain fundamental convictions.

These include the belief that there is a response to the world which may be termed aesthetic awareness, a distinctive perception of the aesthetic dimension of our physical and social environment.

This perception is unique to humankind and has existed as a fundamental part of all human societies from the earliest times. It is through the various arts that this perception of the world is sharpened, enlivened, expressed, and developed as a celebration of life in all its forms.

Cultivation of this awareness is a societal good as it quickens the experience of life and enhances its quality. Thus, the condition of the arts is an appropriate concern of government. In recognition of this fact, The National Endowment for the Arts was created.

It is not the intention of this statement to define "art." The term is to be understood in its broadest sense; that is, with full cognizance of the pluralistic nature of the arts in America, with a deliberate decision to disclaim any endorsement of an "official" arts, and with a full commitment to artistic freedom.[30]

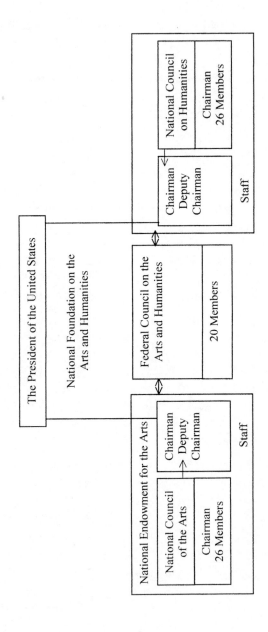

Figure 1. Organizational Structure of the National Foundation on the Arts and the Humanities. *Source: U.S. Government Manual*, 1979–1980, p. 605.

Notes

1. National Endowment for the Arts, *Creative America: Arts and the Pursuit of Happiness* (Washington, D.C.: U.S. Government Printing Office, 1976), p. 8.

2. *Ibid.*, p. 10.

3. *Ibid.*, p. 23.

4. In 1964, The Commission of Fine Arts presented to the president its 18th Report, which covered activities during the period 1 July 1958, to June 1963. The report clarified the following: "As an advisory agency, the Commission cannot force agencies to consult it or take its advice, but it is unable to fulfill its duties if not consulted. Some of the members of the Congress had come to realize the difficulties experienced by the Commission and resolutions (S.J. Res. 147 and H.J. Res. 544, 86th Congress) were introduced by Senator J. William Fulbright of Arkansas and Congressman Frank Thompson of New Jersey, which would give congressional sanction to the jurisdiction of the Commission over the National Capital Region, and which would combine the various Executive Orders of the Commission into a single law. While not making compliance with the Commission's advice mandatory, the proposed legislation . . . required reports to the President and Congress justifying noncompliance with the advice."

5. *Creative America: Arts and the Pursuit of Happiness,* National Endowment for the Arts, Washington, D.C., 1976, p. 22–23.

6. See *Art In America* (May–June 1979), "Issues and Comment." Adding more clarity to the growth and development of the arts agency at this point, it reported that "The National Arts Policy in the second half of the twentieth century was launched in 1960 by Nelson Rockefeller when he was governor of New York, and run, in its first few years, pretty much out of his pocket as a pale shadow of the family's Rockefeller Foundation" (p. 10).

7. Roger L. Stevens also served as Chairman of the Endowment during its initial stages of development. He later became the director of the Kennedy Center for the Performing Arts in Washington, D.C.

8. In 1964, both Houses of the Congress passed legislation approving an Advisory Council on the Arts. President Johnson signed Public Law 88-579 on 3 September 1963, establishing the National Council on the Arts, an advisory body of twenty-four citizens prominent in the arts who were given the responsibility for recommending ways to maintain and increase the cultural resources of the nation.

9. *The National Endowment for the Arts: National Council on the Arts,* "Chairman's Statement," Annual Report, 1975.

10. The Declaration of Purpose for the National Foundation on the Arts and Humanities Act of 1965, Section 2, stated, "The Congress hereby finds and declares . . . (5) That while no government can call a great artist or scholar into existence, it is necessary and appropriate for the federal government to help create and sustain not only a climate encouraging freedom of thought, imagination, and inquiry, but also the material conditions facilitating the release

of this creative talent; (6) That the world leadership which has come to the United States cannot rest solely upon superior power, wealth, and technology, but must be solidly founded upon worldwide respect and admiration for the nation's high qualities as a leader in the realm of ideas and of the spirit; and (7) That, in order to implement these findings, it is desirable to establish a National Foundation on the Arts and Humanities.

11. Nancy Hanks is a graduate of Duke University in Political Science. Prior to her appointment as Chairperson, she spent more than a dozen years working in philanthropy. Ms. Hanks also worked as Nelson Rockefeller's personal secretary during this period. For more details about philanthropy in the arts, see Faye Levine's *The Cultural Barons: An Analysis of Power and Money in the Arts* (New York: Thomas Y. Crowell Co., 1976).

12. See *Chronicle of Higher Education*, "Bill Enacted, Appropriations for the Department of the Interior for Fiscal 1980 provides $154.5 million for the National Endowment for the Arts" (11 February 1980), p. 16.

13. The projected budgets were revealed by the chairman of the budget subcommittee. See, *Washington International Arts Letter*, July-August 1979, p. 2225.

14. See *National Endowment for the Arts: Guide to Programs*, 1979.

15. The Endowment's Education Program is not open to general application. The Endowment does not give grants directly to artists or schools. Matching grants are awarded to state arts agencies and a few other organizations, which administer the Artists-in-Schools Program and select the artists and the sites that will participate.

16. Descriptions for the various Endowment programs were obtained from the *National Endowment for the Arts; Guide to Programs*, 1979.

17. *Annual Report, National Endowment for the Arts, National Council on the Arts*, 1978.

18. See *Washington International Arts Letter*, "Congress Investigation Completed," July–August 1979, p. 2222.

19. *Ibid.*

20. *Ibid.*

21. *Ibid.*

22. See *Washington International Arts Letter*, "Directory of Panelists and Consultants: National Endowment for the Arts," Vol. XVII, No. 5, 158th Letter, May 1978.

23. *Ibid.*

24. Malcom N. Carter in *Arts News*, "The National Endowment for the Arts Grows Up," 78, no. 7, September 1979, p. 61.

25. *Ibid.*, p. 60.

26. "Congress Investigation Completed".

27. *Ibid.*, p. 2224.

28. *Ibid.*

29. Glueck, Grace, "Record Budget for Arts Gain," *New York Times*, (12 May 1977), p. 26C.

30. See *National Endowment for the Arts: Guide to Programs*, "Statement of Goals and Policies," Preamble, p. 39.

Chapter 2

The NEA and the Government

In recent years, there has been a growing increase in both awareness of and concern about the funding of the arts in America.[1] Representatives from cultural institutions and organizations have asserted themselves more aggressively as they have tried to influence legislators who formulate and evaluate legislation related to the appropriation and allocation of funds for the arts. The increased needs, awareness, and concerns for the state of the arts have provoked interest in the traditional "non-arts" oriented public sector.

In 1975, Congressman Fred Richmond (D-NY) introduced legislation[2] in the United States Congress that, if passed, would have opened up the possibility for additional funding for the arts. It was a popular belief within the arts community that the bill would generate millions of dollars for the National Endowment for the Arts and subsequently more funds for arts institutions and organizations across the nation. The bill did not pass however. On the other hand, the thrust did not die.

After Jimmy Carter became President, he appointed Joan Mondale (wife of Vice President Walter Mondale) to head the new administration's program for special concerns of the arts.[3] This gesture by the President satisfied, to some extent, the general concerns of the broader arts community in America. Another voiced concern of the President were his statements regarding changes in racial, ethnic, and gender composition of the Endowment and its implications with regard to funding for various groups, organizations, and individuals.[4] Supposedly, there was to be an effort on the part of the Carter administration to see what was needed or desirable for a more representative and effective Endowment and to work toward bringing about the necessary changes.

The Carter administration, the Endowment, and arts institutions and organizations adopted a number of measures to clarify these voiced concerns. In 1976, the Congressional Black Caucus formed a special committee within its body to devote attention to the funding of black institutions and organizations, and black representation on the Endowment's many panels and programs.[5]

After the Caucus established the committee, several strategy sessions were held in Washington, D.C., with Caucus members, the National Ad Hoc Committee on African-American Contribution to the Arts, and members from various black institutions and organizations from across the nation. The central issues were (1) inequitable distribution of federal arts and humanities funding to minority programs, (2) the slim allotment of contracts to minority firms, and (3) increase in the number of top level minorities at the Endowment.

After Nancy Hanks resigned as Chairman of the Endowment in 1977, President Carter nominated Livingston Biddle, Jr., as her successor. The selection of Biddle to replace Nancy Hanks initially caused considerable political debate in Washington. Basically, the core of the debate stemmed from the charges that the selection of Endowment staff had become very political. It is known in the Washington, D.C., political arena that Senator Clairborne Pell (D-RI) was the most influential individual on Capitol Hill in the area of the arts.[6] There were charges that the selection of Biddle had as much to do with his boyhood relationship with Senator Pell as it had to do with his qualifications for the position. In fact, Michael Straight, former acting chairman of the NEA was quoted in two separate *New York Times* articles as making his feelings known. Straight charged that "the selection of Biddle puts the Endowment in grave danger of being politicized."[7] He also charged that Biddle's appointment was a political payoff for being "Senator Pell's old college roommate."[8]

It was also pointed out in the *New York Times* article that a very strong challenger to Biddle for the position was Peggy Cooper, founder and developer of the Duke Ellington High School of the Performing Arts/Workshops for Careers in the Arts. Ms. Cooper was quoted as saying that "she believed that opposition to her came from 'big art'— the old, established organizations, because of her commitment to 'community programming.'"[9] She also "suggested that the arts establishment is not yet ready for a Chairman who is young and black."[10] The writer of the article went on to confirm some of Ms. Cooper's contentions by pointing out that "several people who direct large organizations voiced negative views about Miss Cooper's candidacy."[11] He wrote that the director of one such institution said, "Everybody was terrified of her."[12]

In August of 1979, the House Appropriations Committee leveled serious charges against the Endowment and its operation procedures.[13] The Committee released a report that questioned the NEA's ability to perform, its fairness, and its commitment to its legislative mandate. The House Appropriations Subcommittee on Interior released the study after a nine-month investigation of the Endowment. Some of the conclusions of investigation even prompted some of those who authorized it to denounce its findings. The report concluded the following:

(1) The NEA operates with poor management procedures;

(2) The NEA abrogated its leadership role and allowed project application to become a surrogate national policy, shaping the program of the Endowment;

(3) The composition of task, committees, panels and consultant teams is, at best, a study in the repetitive use of the same individuals. . . . The "close circle" also provides the appearance of, and possibly the fact of, favoritism in awards; and

(4) The NEA cannot make a fair or informed quality judgment or reflect the plurality that is art in America.

Although the NEA chairman dismissed the charges in the report as being inaccurate, he maintained that "it required us to do a great deal of soul-searching."[14]

The Endowment maintained that one of its primary concerns was to perpetuate "cultural pluralism." It has professed full "cognizance of the pluralistic nature of the arts in America." However, one might wonder about the Endowment's concept of "full cognizance" and its relationship to programming. Vantile Whitfield, former Director of Expansion Arts at the Endowment, commenting on the slices of the federal, state, and municipal budget pies, argued that

Infinitely smaller fractions of these slices are doled out to the isolated, indigenous art forms; the largest portions of these slices are seemingly predestined for "major institutions" in the arts. It is common knowledge that most of these "major institutions" exist primarily to preserve and glorify European art only.[15]

With the bulk of the Endowment's budget going to "major institutions," testifying before the House Appropriations Committee on the 1980 budget for the Endowment, Shirley Chisholm, Chairperson of the Congressional Black Caucus' Braintrust on the Arts and the Humanities called for a plan by which language in the NEA's budget would stress that "demonstrating a plan for increased access to funding by minorities and other underrepresented groups."[16] She also "sharply criticized the NEA for inequitable distribution of federal arts funding to minority programs and the slim allotment of contracts to minority firms."[17] Congressperson Chisholm also emphasized the need to increase the number of top-level minorities at the Endowment. She concluded her testimony by stating, "Realizing the historic contributions which blacks and Hispanics have made to America's cultural expression, it is inconceivable that only five percent is estimated to have been awarded to minority groups."[18]

Perhaps in defense of the NEA's programs and processes, some overtones concerning these and other issues were prevalent in a speech by the Endowment's Chairman, Livingston L. Biddle, Jr. Biddle stated that

> We find words like "elitism" and "populism" being used to suggest a polarization of the arts. Some suggest that elitism applies to the quality of our major arts institutions, our orchestras, our opera companies, our dance and theater organizations, our museums. And some suggest that "populism" applies to an opposite and perhaps equally separate domain—the state and local organizations which represent the arts at the grassroots. And some even suggest that lines should be drawn and alternatives chosen.
>
> I am convinced of a very different means of defining our cultural goals. It seems to me that "elitism" can indeed mean quality, can indeed mean "the best"—that is a proper dictionary meaning for the word. And "populism" I would suggest can mean "access." Access to the arts all across the land. Why not bridge these two words—why not join them in harmony, rather than in discord?—and simply say that together they can mean "access to the best."[19]

This kind of "rationale" was being contested at the Endowment level. Just what does "access to the best" really mean? Furthermore, *who* determines *what* is "the best?" Because the term *best* is relative, what are the processes for determining, objectively, *what* and *who* is "best"? Then, of course, the question must always be kept in mind, best for whom? These particular questions are addressed in the next two chapters.

An issue of *Grassroots and Pavement* presented a reflection of NEA in "Roundtable With: The NEA Leadership." The article stated,

> The National Endowment for the Arts (NEA) is in the business of supporting the advancement of the American cultural legacy. It is a monumental task undertaken by a federal agency which, throughout its history, has been plagued by budget limitations. On the one hand, NEA has to defend against allegations of being too "elitist," and too "populist" on the other. While balancing these charges, it has to provide cultural enrichment, foster educational awareness, promote human services and nurture civic values.
>
> The fact that NEA's mandate is unclear to many Americans stems from basic misconceptions about the arts. A number of stereotypes and generalizations have been applied against people in the arts, practitioners and patrons alike, as well as against cultural institutions and arts support organizations.
>
> The NEA's constituents are all Americans—rich and poor, ethnic majorities and minorities, young and old, urban and rural. The arts touch every facet of American life. They are an expression of cultural values. . . . As the NEA continues to expand, the controversies will continue to grow. Public appeal breeds public opinion.[20]

From their perspectives, the administrators at the top levels within the Endowment presented their views as follows.

Mary Ann Tighe, Deputy Chairman for Programs, stated,

> No single person knows what "art" is, and the Endowment has to be very aware of that fact. You know, there has always been that feeling among the public that we're the arts, and that most of our judgment are subjective, having more to do with personal response. Of course, that's true. But I think a lot of times, we at the Endowment have used that as an excuse, without saying clearly why we're doing something. After listening to a lot of people, the need is clearly for us to be able to articulate what we're doing and to be accountable for it. I think we've been working toward that goal.[21]

A. B. Spellman, Director of the Expansion Arts Program asserted,

> The momentum is with neighborhood arts. The neighborhood arts movement is much of the arts landscape. It's like a pyramid and at the base are the neighborhoods. I also think that the concept of

twenty-first century American art is vested in communities. The communities that we (Expansion Arts) support are very, very rich in culture, but very poor in institutions. As we support more organizations which work directly with these cultural sources, we'll find artistic expressions which won't be as monochromatic as the arts of the twentieth century. Look at all that genius that got left out simply because there was nowhere to go.[22]

Gordon Braithwaite, Special Assistant to the Chairman for Minority Concerns argued in a similar vein that

We are trying to reorganize different arts initiatives from all over the nation. We respect their contributions and integrity. The arts used to be viewed as an isolated phenomenon; now we see them as an integral part of our everyday life. For us, culture is a mirror of our nation's legacy.[23]

Another significant aspect of the Endowment is its international program. In 1978, the Endowment expanded its international activities. As reported in the Endowment's *Annual Report* for 1978,

The Endowment and its panels will advise the International Communication Agency (ICA) on international cultural exhibitions and events. In a memorandum of understanding, the White House outlines how the cooperative ventures works. ICA—which was created in 1977 by merging the State Department's Bureau of Cultural Affairs, the United States Information Agency, and the Voice of America—will present the Endowment chairman with "comprehensive lists of overseas opportunities for art exhibitions, performing arts events, speakers, and other types of cultural activities." ICA also will submit a list of organizations, artists, and scholars interested in traveling or sending works abroad. The Endowment's advisory panels will then review the lists and select and rank final choices. Final decisions on specific exchange activities and participants will rest with the director of the ICA.

The Endowment will also provide ICA with lists of their grantees and cultural activities around the United States. . . . As a result, ICA will be continuously posted on arts events in this country.[24]

On the subject of the United States Information Agency (USIA), J. William Fulbright wrote in his book, *The Pentagon Propaganda Machine,*

Although the Department of State is supposedly responsible for cultural exchanges, Defense with State, the United States Information Agency and the White House, sponsored tours of this country by foreign journalists. Between 1966 and 1969, about two hundred of them were brought here from Europe, Africa, South and East Asia, and the Pacific. Transportation within the United States was by military installations.[25]

Given these realities, certain implications are revealed with respect to the role of "cultural politics" and U.S. public policy. As reported in *U.S. News and World Report*, "While America's political prestige may be declining in some areas of the world, this nation's reputation as cultural leader is at an all-time high—and still growing."[26]

Notes

1. The importance of this issue was raised in an article in the *U.S. News and World Report* (8 August 1977). An article titled, "The Cultural Book," pointed out that "all across the nation, theatre, ballet, opera and museums have become smash hits—topping even old favorites such as baseball. It's part of an insatiable market for culture that is transforming America" (p. 50). John Gingrich, President of the Association of American Dance Companies, credited "the National Endowment for the Arts for part of the growth" (p. 53). The article also revealed that "the federally funded National Endowment for the Arts spends $85 million a year on cultural enterprises."

2. Congressman Richmond's Bill (HR 1042) instructs the Internal Revenue Service to place three check-off boxes on the first page of the income tax form to allow the taxpayer to contribute to the arts (via the National Endowment for the Arts), to education (via the National Endowment for the Humanities), or both. One hundred fifty-eight members of Congress signed as cosponsors of the legislation. It is projected that such a bill would generate $1 billion annually.

3. Joan Mondale was appointed Honorary Chairman of the Federal Council on the Arts and Humanities.

4. See *Atlanta Daily World*, "28 U.S. Agencies Directed to Develop Civil Rights Efforts," 5 January 1978. The Department of Justice directed twenty-eight federal departments and agencies to develop plans for the enforcement of a civil rights law to prohibit discrimination in federally assisted programs. President Carter issued a memorandum in July 1977 requesting Attorney General Griffin Bell to monitor certain federal agencies "to make sure that they are 'doing an effective job' in enforcing Title VI of the Civil Rights Act of 1964." The NEA was one of the twenty-eight federal agencies cited. This network of federal agencies operates approximately 400 programs covered by Title VI and dispenses an estimated $70 billion a year in federal funds.

5. The Congressional Black Caucus Braintrust on the Arts and Humanities was headed by Congresswoman Shirley Chisholm (D-NY). The committee also focused attention on the National Endowment for the Humanities and other federal funding agencies. As reported in Congressional Black Caucus' *For the People* (The Caucus' newsletter—Third/Fourth Quarter Legislative Report 1978), "The Chairman of the Arts Endowment, Livingston Biddle, announced the appointment of Gordon Braithwaite as the Chairman's special representative for minority concerns . . . to serve as a liaison and as a developer of policy initiatives which are needed to make the Endowment more responsive to Black concerns" (p. 3). Also see *Black Enterprise* (December 1977), "Feuding, Fussing and Fighting: Funding the Arts in America," in which writer A. Peter Bailey quoted Ellis Haizlip as saying, "Most all of the arts funding decisions on both the public and private levels are being made without any significant contribution from concerned black people" (p. 80).

6. Senator Pell is Chairman of the Senate Subcommittee for Education, Arts, and Humanities. He was first elected to the Senate in 1960.

7. John S. Friedman, "How Nancy Hanks' Successor was Chosen," *New York Times*, 16 October 1977, p. 36D.

8. Robert Brustein, "Whither the National Arts and Humanities Endowment," *New York Times*, 18 December 1977, p. 35D.

9. John S. Friedman, "Nancy Hanks' Successor." One of the particular concerns of the Congressional Black Caucus' Braintrust on the Arts and Humanities has been neighborhood programs. Community programming tends not to be of particular concern to the art establishment. See *Grassroots and Pavements* (GAP) Newsbrief Vol. I, no. 3, "Chisholm Talks Art." Commenting in an interview, Chisholm argued, "The artistic merit of neighborhood arts must be recognized and supported if they are to continue to contribute to the enhancement of community life. Neighborhood arts are often not viewed as 'legitimate arts.' This image must be changed. Community arts must receive the kind of recognition and financial support from established institutions, like the National Endowment for the Arts."

10. John S. Friedman, "Nancy Hanks' Successor," *New York Times*, 16 October 1977, p. 36D.

11. *Ibid.*

12. *Ibid.*

13. The House Appropriations Committee oversees the appropriation and allocation of funds to the Endowment. The committee is chaired by Representative Sidney Yates (D-IL). The committee's investigators (Surveys and Investigation Staff) observed the NEA's operations, policies, programs, and procedures.

14. See *Art News*, "The National Endowment for the Arts Grows Up," 78, no. 7 (1979): p. 59.

15. See *Grassroots and Pavements*, "Linkage Among the Arts," 1, no. 2 (1979).

16. See *Grassroots and Pavements*, "Hill Hearing on the Arts," 1, no. 2 (1979).

17. *Ibid.*

18. *Ibid.*

19. Chairman Biddle made these statements while speaking before a nominating hearing of the Committee on Human Resources of the United States Senate on 2 November 1977.

20. See *Grassroots and Pavement*, "Roundtable With: The NEA Leadership," I, no. 2 (1979).

21. *Ibid.*

22. *Ibid.*

23. *Ibid.*

24. See National Endowment for the Arts, National Council on the Arts, *Annual Report*, 1978, p. 11.

25. J. William Fulbright, *The Pentagon Propaganda Machine* (New York: Liveright, 1970), p. 34.

26. See *U.S. News and World Report*, "The Cultural Boom," 8 August 1977, Planned Parenthood, pp. 50–53.

Chapter 3

The NEA Maze

God forbid we ever have government policy for the arts, per se. That
would remind me of Nazi Germany, or something of that sort, where
the government sets what the policy should be. It should not.

—Senator Clairborne Pell, Chairman of the
Subcommittee on Education, Arts and the
Humanities of the Committee on Labor and
Human Resources, 26 June 1979.

The continued examination of the Endowment produced numerous
"changes" in its operations. This chapter attempts to give adequate
explanations concerning the review process, categorization of the
applications process, staffing procedures and various other procedures
by focusing on certain particular issues. I have given particular attention to Chairman of the Arts Endowment, Livingston Biddle, Jr.'s testimony before the Senate Subcommittee on Education, Arts and Humanities and the Committee on Labor and Human Resources; Chairperson
of the Congressional Black Caucus' Braintrust on the Arts and the
Humanities, Congresswoman Shirley Chisholm's testimony before the
House Appropriations Subcommittee on Interior; Special Assistant to
the Endowment Chairman for the Minority Concerns, Gordon
Braithwaite's presentation to The Southern Regional Black Arts Conference held at The Atlanta University Center in October (1979);
NEA's 1978 Challenge Grant Awards; and the National Assembly of
State Arts Agencies and their relationship to the Endowment, and
"small groups and struggling artists."

The decisions that are made at the Endowment concerning grants
and applications take place within various panels. During this exam-

ination, many criticisms arose concerning the panel system. One reaction to the various criticisms came from Endowment Chairman Livingston Biddle, Jr. On 6 April 1978, he sent out a memorandum to "All Endowment Staff and All Parties Concerned" with the subject, "Rotation Policy."

Biddle took the opportunity to explain that since his appointment (November 1977), he had had numerous discussions with program directors, the National Council on the Arts, and other leaders in the arts community. As a result of these discussions, he was proposing that a number of "changes" be made to the structure of the Endowment. To accomplish these changes, he appointed three additional deputy chairmen. He explained this change by stating that

> The appointment of three Deputy Chairmen—rather than the one in previous years—was motivated by a desire to make the Endowment as responsive as possible, in our major areas of interest and endeavor, to the changing and mounting needs of the arts and the growing demands on the Endowment.[1]

Biddle pointed out that he felt that the Endowment had the immense responsibility to keep the arts evolving. He argued that "the Endowment had served as a catalyst in accord with its mandate."[2] This particular issue is one that the Endowment has had to confront consistently. The question of whether or not the Endowment has fulfilled its legislative mandate is one that has not been clearly answered by all responsible parties.

Biddle further explained the changes that were being proposed as follows:

> With respect to the Chairman, the Council, and the Panels, rotation is a part of our historic development and basic philosophy. And I believe this philosophy should apply to the positions of our Program Directors. In some important respects, their positions are the most sensitive of all. No Chairman, no Deputy, no single Council Member, no Panelist, can be fully knowledgeable in all fields of the arts. The Program Directors, however, have a special responsibility, a special proximity to the major art forms. Special reliance is placed on their abilities. The principle of rotation, in my view, would be incomplete without their involvement in the process.[3]

Biddle also expressed his feelings that no one, regardless of their position, should serve within the Endowment forever. He called for a rotation system with principle and fairness. He indicated that "within the principle of rotation . . . each program area and its leadership should be carefully assessed year by year. No arbitrary kind of uniformity should apply."[4] Biddle also revealed that his intent was to make the Arts Endowment "an increasing resource for all fields"[5] and to those who work at the Endowment. These were the basic concerns raised by Biddle. However, two very specific issues were not raised in his memorandum. Who or what positions would be rotated? What, if any, was the relationship between (1) a rotating policy, (2) "an increasing resource for all fields," and (3) an increasing resource for all ethnic and racial groups?

Another response to the charges raised against the Endowment came from one of the deputy directors. Under the direction of Deputy Director of Programs Mary Ann Tighe, the Endowment conducted a self-study to evaluate its operation. In late 1978, the study was completed. As a result of this study, many reforms were recommended, and a number of measures were proposed. Endowment Chairman Livingston Biddle, Jr., testified on 26 June 1979 before the Senate Subcommittee on Education, Arts, and Humanities of the Committee on Labor and Human Resources on a bill to reauthorize the National Endowment for the Arts. He presented to the committee the Endowment's recommendations for change. He stated, "The study recommended that each program have a standing policy panel and grant panels whose duties would be limited to application review and specific recommendations arising from application review. Previously, there were no standing policy panels."[6]

The study found an overburdened system with larger and larger application loads that tended to stretch out the time of panel meetings, making them more and more exhausting and time-consuming and less productive. Most of the time in meetings had to be spent on application review, which necessitated abbreviation of important discussions on policy. As the areas of Endowment support grow more and more sophisticated within a given art form, panelists with specialized information were required, which often swelled the size of panel. A panel that was too large for good discussion, though, seemed to be too small to provide all of the firsthand information needed for grant making. Information had not kept pace with increasing applications in several fields. More site visits were needed to provide reliable firsthand information on new applicants who had never been seen and grantees who had not been seen for some time.

A program's policy panel would consist of twelve to fifteen panelists, including a state arts agency representative, and would represent a broad range of professional and aesthetic viewpoints with as much cultural, ethnic, and regional distribution as is feasible. The panel would comprise a group of "experts" who had some experience with the Endowment's grant-making procedures. As with all Endowment panelists, the panelists are approved year by year, serving on the policy panel for a maximum of three years. The policy panel would rotate off by thirds, changing completely every three years.

The policy panel develops program directions and guidelines, reviews and recommends budget allocations, proposes and helps develop pilot projects, and reviews applications under the program's pilot projects.

A program's grant panel would then be composed of grant panelists and one or more members of the policy panel. Together with the specific expertise needed, grant panels would provide broad representation in all respects, including professional, regional, cultural, and aesthetic. All panelists at the Endowment are appointed for one-year terms, and policy panelists could be reappointed for a maximum two consecutive years. About half of the people on all grant panels would rotate off each year, to give more of the field an opportunity to participate in and learn about the Endowment process.

In proposing these structural changes, it was the Endowment's belief that this two-tiered system of policy and grant panel procedure would have a major impact on improving the quality and fairness of decision-making. Separating policy discussions from grant review is a way of more clearly defining function, and the new system provided the necessary linkage between policy and grant function. Moreover, a growing workload is shared among a greater number of participants who in aggregate would also provide broader representation from the field. Biddle later responded to a House Appropriations Committee report that was very critical of the Endowment and stated that "We believe that the peer panel review system does well in evaluating the past and potential performance of individual artists or arts organizations. We are not so successful in evaluating the impact of our total program activities."[7] Furthermore, Biddle commented that under his leadership, the Endowment had "made specific efforts...to examine the panel system and make it" more responsive that it was before."[8] Changes were recognized by *Art in America*, which stated that "reorganization of its panel system has had the effect of firming up its policy hierarchy. Now programs all have standing policy panels with all panelists chairing smaller, specialized grant panels in their field. All NEA panelists will now be issued a handbook that details Endowment policies, operations and panelist responsibilities; they will also receive more formal orientation."[9]

Testifying on 8 May 1979 before the House Appropriations Subcommittee on Interior, Chairperson of the Congressional Black Caucus' Braintrust on the Arts and the Humanities, Congresswoman Shirley Chisholm, raised sharp criticisms of the Endowment. She stated that there were a number of serious issues that needed to be addressed by the Endowment. She raised concerns over the fact that there were various programs at the Endowment that awarded no money to minority applicants. She cited specific examples, including the Media Arts and Museum programs. Another aspect of her testimony focused on the lack of grants to black colleges, while at the same time, millions of dollars are awarded to other postsecondary institutions. She emphasized that only four minority firms had received contract grants from the Endowment.

The testimony criticized the lack of minorities in managerial positions at the Endowment. She stated that of approximately eighty minority employees, forty-four (or fifty-five percent) were concentrated in clerical positions from GS-1 to GS-7 (see Table 3). She pointed out that only five minorities were included in the total of 325 that made up the NEA's management, and of those five, only three had direct authority over programs. She criticized the Endowment for its lack of minorities in policy-making roles. She pointed out that the Endowment approach to these concerns was to create what is called the Office of Minority Concerns. She argued that this gesture did not even begin to address the existing problems. She concluded her testimony by making several recommendations to the subcommittee (see Appendix A for complete text).

Table 4, below, reflects the basic interest in dollar amounts of the NEA's 1978 Challenge Grant program.

Table 3. NEA Employees: Federal Job Grade Breakdown

Grade	Full-time	Part-time	Temporary
GS-1	0	0	0
GS-2	0	2	3
GS-3	0	3	2
GS-4	2	10	10
GS-5	13	21	0
GS-6	11	6	0

Table 3, Cont'd.

Grade	Full-time	Part-time	Temporary
GS-7	30	25	0
GS-8	5	0	0
GS-9	36	9	0
GS-10	1	0	0
GS-11	29	4	0
GS-12	24	2	0
GS-13	17	0	0
GS-15	24	0	0
GS-16	1	0	0
GS-17	2	0	0
GS-18	1	0	0
Executive Level	1	0	0
Total	216	83	25

Source: *Arts, Humanities, and Museum Services Act of 1979.* Hearings before the Subcommittee on Education, Arts and Humanities of the Committee on Labor and Human Resources, United States Senate, 96th Congress, 1st Sess. on S. 1386, June 26, 27, and 28, 1979, p. 82.

Table 4. 1978 NEA Challenge Grant Awards

Institution and Organizations	Amount Awarded
National Symphony Orchestra (Washington, D.C.)	$1,000,000
Metropolitan Opera Association (New York City)	1,500,000
Musical Arts Association (Cleveland Orchestra)	1,000,000
Carnegie Institute of Pittsburgh Symphony Society, Inc.	2,000,000
Detroit Symphony Orchestra	1,000,000
Lyric Opera of Chicago	600,000
Saint Louis Symphony Society	1,000,000
Baltimore Symphony Orchestra	600,000
Boston Symphony	850,000
Dallas Symphony Orchestra	450,000

Table 4, Cont'd.

Institution and Organizations	Amount
Denver Symphony Orchestra	450,000
Minnesota Orchestra Association	750,000
New York City Opera	700,000
Orchestral Association/Chicago Symphony	1,000,000
Rochester Philharmonic (New York)	450,000
San Francisco Opera	750,000
San Francisco Symphony Association	750,000
Seattle Opera Association	350,000
Seattle Symphony	600,000
Houston Grand Opera Association	500,000
Utah Symphony	365,000
Museum of Modern Art (New York City)	1,000,000
Lincoln Center for the Performing Arts (New York City)	500,000
The City Center of Music and Drama (New York City Ballet)	1,000,000
Brooklyn Institute of Arts and Science (New York)	1,000,000
Baltimore Museum of Art	800,000
Performing Arts Center of the Music Center of Los Angeles	2,040,000
Sponsors of the San Francisco Performing Arts Center, Inc.	1,000,000
Ballet Theatre Foundation/American Ballet Theatre (New York City)	1,000,000
Cincinnati Institute of Fine Art	2,000,000
Carnegie Hall Society	750,000
Guggenheim (Solomon R.) Museum	1,000,000
Minnesota Public Radio	500,000
New York Shakespeare Festival	450,000
Philharmonic Symphony Society of New York	850,000
Whitney Museum of American Art (New York City)	750,000
Foundation for the Joffrey Ballet, Inc. (New York City)	450,000

Source: National Endowment for the Arts, National Council on the Arts, *Annual Report* 1978. See section titled "Challenge Grants," pp. 56–68.

Because much of Congresswoman Shirley Chisholm's testimony focused on the Office of Minority Concerns, it is indeed important to this discussion that some light be shed on the function of this office. Gordon Braithwaite, Special Assistant to the Chairman of the Endowment, spoke to the Southern Regional Black Arts Conference on 13 October 1979, in Atlanta, Georgia. He made the following statement:

> For the last year, I've been a part of something called Special Assistant to the Chairman for Minority Concerns, sometimes called the Office of Minority Concerns. As you can see, I'm not an office. So if some of you are confused by the capacities or the unevenness of the capability during the last year, as you have approached the Office of Minority Concerns, it is because it is comprised of myself and a clerk-typist. She is overwhelmingly at your service, but we can only do so much. We do have with us an EEO officer who is an individual at all of the federal agencies, and she and her secretary have worked diligently to complement some of the things that we need to do for you. But this is what the Office of Minority Concerns is primarily comprised of.
>
> We were joined by Joe Rodriguez four months ago who specifically was put aboard to attend the needs of the Hispanic Task Force, which has been convening for the last year. So that's the show. . . .
>
> For four years, I was with the Expansion Arts Program, which was the primary, and still becomes the primary program for funding most of your projects. That program—expansion arts—is now headed by A. B. Spellman. And then for two years, I was head of a program called "Special Projects," and then recently I was asked to have the dubious honor of addressing minority concerns in the country for my chairman.
>
> It's dubious because I don't know if everyone wants to hear about it every day, and that's how often we need to talk about it. It is a primary concern of mine and of yours, and hopefully of the agency where I work, but the communication isn't always there. I've sort of been one of those people that has been the cart before the horse, and it has occurred to me that for the last few days that you are the horse. . . .
>
> I have so little opportunity to speak on an intimate basis with black people around the country, that I must honestly say that I am requesting that the whites think of themselves as blacks so that none of you will think that I am being hostile. Because I do have some things to say that I perceive as being hostile, and they are not—they are just my concerns for the black people.

If we understand that nothing has happened, we won't be so discouraged. Because as I look at the picture nationally, as I look at what we're discussing from day to day, nothing has really happened.[10]

Perhaps this is the very same reality to which Congresswoman Shirley Chisholm alluded in her testimony to the House Appropriations Subcommittee when she pointed out that, even though the Justice Department and the Endowment's General Counsel had recommended hiring of a Compliance Officer (an Equal Employment Specialist), the Endowment instead froze the position. Although White House officials gave lip service to altering the structure and practices at the Endowment, things "changed" but yet they remained the same. The Endowment's approach to the problems that have been cited here was to shift people around in various positions. Congresswoman Chisholm stated in her testimony that she was aware of the Investigations Staff Report to the NEA that recommended reorganization of its panel structure. However, she also stated, that:

Although I believe that this would enhance the diversity of the review process, I feel it does not go to the core issue: Who will be responsible for overseeing access and equity in the Endowment's programs?"[11]

Notes

1. See *Arts, Humanities, and Museum Service Act of 1979.* Hearing Before the Subcommittee on Education, Arts, and Humanities of the Committee on Labor and Human Resources: United States Senate, 96th Congress, 1st Sess. on S. 1386, 26, 27, and 28 June 1979, p. 63.

2. *Ibid.*

3. *Ibid.*

4. *Ibid.*, p. 65.

5. *Ibid.*

6. *Ibid.*, p. 113.

7. Carter, Malcolm N., in *Arts News*, "The National Endowment for the Arts Grows Up," *78*, no. 7, September 1979, p. 60.

8. *Ibid.*

9. Robinson, Walter, in *Arts in America, Issues and Commentary*, "Politicians and Arts: Eyes on the NEA," 1979, p. 13.

10. These statements were made at The Southern Regional Black Arts Conference, sponsored by the Southern Arts Federation, Atlanta University Center, 11–13 October, 1979.

11. Hearing Before the Subcommittee on Education, Arts, and Humanities of the Committee on Labor and Human Resources, p. 63.

Chapter 4

The NEA and the Politics of Culture

To quote Bernard Shaw, "Next to torture, art persuades fastest." Art is the best therapy. Men all through the ages have known this. Scientists are admitting this now. Art is the best means of education—the church has always known this; our colleges and civic bodies are learning it. Art is the best means of communication. The church has known this too: the State Department is learning it.

> Agnes DeMille, choreographer and former member of the National Council on the Arts, in testimony presented to the Senate Subcommittee on Education, Art and the Humanities, 26 June 1979

Just what is the existing aesthetic in America? How is it shaped, formed, and maintained? Furthermore, what is the relationship of the National Endowment for the Arts in helping to shape and maintain those values? The Endowment has consistently defended itself against those who have argued that it is elitist and is basically unconcerned with popular art expressions. Based on certain identifiable realities, the Endowment indeed has established a systematic pattern for staffing of personnel and awarding of grants that tends more to support the charges against the NEA than they do to support the replies by the Endowment.

Congresswoman Shirley Chisholm pointed out in a testimony before the House Appropriations Subcommittee that there are programs at the NEA from which blacks and other minorities receive absolutely no support for their activities.[1] She also pointed out that most of the minority staff members at the Endowment were in the lower-level (GS-1 to GS-7) clerical positions.

The Endowment has been irresponsible in its obligation to enforce Civil Rights requirements. It refused to act on recommendations of the

Justice Department and its own General Counsel to hire a Compliance Officer to help ensure equal employment opportunities for its staff. The allocation of grants is reflected in the staffing pattern. The Endowment grants to black applicants are awarded primarily from one of the inter-disciplinary programs (Expansion Arts) and not from one of the eight specific arts disciplines. Note also that the bulk of the funding to black institutions and organizations has come from the budget that has been set aside under the category of Expansion Arts. However, all of the other institutions and organizations that apply to the Endowment either also receive funds from this particular category or they are eligible to do so. The same is not true with respect to blacks. There is no evidence to indicate that any black institution or organization has consistently benefited from the NEA's various programs or disciplines. The established pattern at the Endowment reflects a "system of apartheid" both in staffing and in grant allocation.

The previous chapter cited 1978 Challenge Grant Awards. Particular attention should be given to the fact that in this program, millions of dollars are awarded to a few institutions and organizations (basically for symphonies and opera). This evidence tends to support the charges raised by Representative Yates that the Endowment finances "only established groups."[2] In light of the "diversity of cultures" in America, what is the rationale behind granting these select few institutions and organizations millions and millions of dollars on the one hand, and other types of institutions and organizations a few pennies or nothing? The Museum of Natural History, Lincoln Center for the Performing Arts, and the Philharmonic Symphony Society of New York are all New York City–based institutions and organizations that the NEA funds consistently on an annual basis with millions and millions of dollars. Why? In the state of California, the following institutions and organizations fall into this category: The Los Angeles Philharmonic Association's Performing Arts Council of the Music Center of Los Angeles, Inc.; Los Angeles Institute of Contemporary Art; San Francisco Opera Association; San Francisco Symphony Association; Sponsors of the San Francisco Performing Arts Center, Inc.; San Francisco Museum of Modern Art; and San Francisco Ballet Association.

In 1974, The John F. Kennedy Center for the Performing Arts (Washington, D.C.) received a grant in the amount of $253,000 from the Endowment. In 1977 certain issues were raised concerning blacks being excluded by the Kennedy Center. The criticism was that although the Center is located in a city that is predominately black and receives public funds for operation, its program and activities tend to appeal to a particular population segment of the Washington, D.C., area. As a result of what were identified as clear cases of nonparticipation and involvement on the part of blacks in the Center's activities, a special committee was formed to monitor this situation.[3] This particular kind of problem relates directly to the Endowment and reflects the fact that the NEA has been irresponsible in monitoring the practices of its grantees, although it is required by law to do so.

In addition to these concerns raised about the Endowment, in June of 1978, an article appeared in the *Atlanta Constitution* titled, "How the South Gets Gypped." The writer of the article, Helen C. Smith, started by saying,

> There is a great big lucious pie, concocted out of taxpayers' green stuff, up in Washington at the National Endowment for the Arts, that is sliced into tempting morsels that feed the spirit through the arts.[4]

From this point, she raised the question, "But are those slices divided equitably?"[5] More specifically, "Is the south the stepchild who gets an occasional crumb instead of the whole feast?"[6] Smith raised three particular points of interest:

(1) The per capita amount of NEA funds allocated for 1977–1978 to the five existing regional arts agencies were:

Western	$3.19
Mid-American	$2.48
Upper Midwest	$1.78
New England	$ .82
Southeastern	$ .81[7]

(2) Staffing for panelists, Challenge Grant allocations, and percentage of the dollars were disproportionately distributed (Table 5).

Table 5. Distribution of Panelists, Grants, and Dollars Allocated (%)[8]

	Panelists	Challenge Grants	% of Total Dollars
Northeast	51	49	49
Other	30	30	30
California	12	10	13
South	7	10	9

(3) Although the Southern region constitutes twenty percent of the population, it only benefits about seven percent worth in resources. The article quoted Anthony Turney, Executive Director of the Southern Arts Federation as saying,

> Looking at the NEA annual report for 1976, it shows that 464 citizens sat on the various advisory panels that make recommendations to the National Council on the Arts. Of those 464 citizens, only 33 came from the South. . . . I cannot help but ponder on the fact that there is a similarity between the percentages of grants, dollars and panelists as they pertain to the South . . . (and) there is a similar correlation between the large Northeastern and California representation.[9]

What these figures demonstrate is that there is a disproportionate representation on the Endowment's staff, as well as a disproportionate allocation in grants. This particular system of unequal distribution is based solely on personal and geographic interests. The West (primarily California) and the Northeast (primarily New York City) tend to be at the top of the Endowment's priorities. Once these two areas are satisfied, the scramble takes place to divide whatever else is left over. This is the case whether the issue is per capita funding, appointment of panelists, number and amount of grants, or percentage of dollar amounts. This situation exists because of the Endowment's allegiance to certain individuals who have close relationships with certain cultural institutions and organizations. What are some of these institutions and organizations?

In Thomas R. Dye's *Who's Running America?*, the author focused on the issue of "The Cultural Organizations." He wrote, "The identification of the nation's leading . . . cultural institutions requires qualitative judgment about the prestige and influence of a variety of organizations."[10] He selected six cultural organizations:

> The Metropolitan Museum of Art,
> The Smithsonian Institution,
> Museum of Modern Art,
> Lincoln Center for the Performing Arts,
> National Gallery of Art, and
> John F. Kennedy Center for the Performing Arts.

Dye stated,

> It is difficult to measure the power of particular institutions in the world of art, music, and theatre. Certainly there are a number of vi-

able alternatives that might be added to or substituted for our choices.[6]

The *Metropolitan Museum of Art* in New York City is the largest museum in the United States, with a collection of nearly one-half million objects of art. Decisions of the Metropolitan Museum regarding exhibitions, collections, showings, and art objects have tremendous impact on what is or is not to be considered valued art in America. These decisions are the formal responsibility of the governing board. This board includes names such as

Arthur A. Houghton, President and Chairman of the Board of Corning Glass;

C. Douglas Dillon, former Secretary of Treasury, Under Secretary of State, and a Director of Chase Manhattan Bank; and

Mrs. McGeorge Bundy, wife of the former presidential assistant for national security affairs under Presidents Kennedy and Johnson and former president of the Ford Foundation.

The Smithsonian Institution in Washington, D.C., supports a wide variety of scientific publications, collections, and exhibitions. It also exercised nominal control over the National Gallery of Art, the John F. Kennedy Center for the Performing Arts, and the Museum of Natural History, although these component organizations have their own boards of directors. The Smithsonian itself is directed by a board that consists of the vice president of the United States, the Chief Justice of the Supreme Court, three U.S. Senators, three U.S. Representatives, and six "private citizens," including

Crawford Greenwalt, former Chairman of the Board of E. I. DuPont De Nemours and a trustee of the DuPont's Christiana Securities Corporation and Morgan Guaranty Trust Company;

Thomas J. Watson, Jr., Chairman of the Board of IBM;

William A. M. Burden, a descendant of the Vanderbilts of New York City and investor in and director of Allied Chemicals, CBS, Lockheed Aircraft, Manufacturers Hanover Trust, and American Metal Climax, who also has served as ambassador to Belgium;

Carl P. Haskins, President of the Carnegie Foundation and a trustee of the Council on Foreign Relations, RAND Corporation; and

James Edwin Webb, former director of the U.S. Bureau of the Budget and Under Secretary of State, former director of the National Aeronautics and Space Administration, a director of Kerr McGee Oil Corporation and Sperry Rand, and trustee of the Committee for Economic Development;

The National Gallery of Art is the capital's leading art institution. It was founded in 1937 when Andrew W. Mellon made the original donation of his art collection together with $15 million to build the gallery itself. Since then, it has accepted other collections from wealthy philanthropists and exercises considerable influence in the art world. As of 1979 its directors included

Paul Mellon, a son of Andrew Mellon and a director of Mellon National Bank and Trust and the Kellon Foundation;

John Hay Whitney, centimillionaire, former publisher of the *New York Herald Tribune* and ambassador to Great Britain; and

Stoddard M. Stevens, senior partner, Sullivan and Cromwell, top Wall Street law firm.

The John F. Kennedy Center for the Performing Arts in Washington, D.C., which was begun in 1964, also has had considerable influence on the arts in America. Its board is largely political in origin:

Arthur Ochs Sulzberger, publisher and president of the *New York Times*; and

Henry S. Morgan, son of J. P. Morgan, who founded U. S. Steel Corporation and International Harvester and became one of the world's wealthiest men in the 1920s through his control of Morgan Guaranty Bank.

The Museum of Modern Art in New York City is the leading institution in the nation devoted to collecting and exhibiting contemporary art. It houses not only paintings and sculpture, but also films, prints, and photography. Its loan exhibitions circulate art works throughout the world. The determination of what is to be considered "art" in the world of modern art is extremely subjective. The directors of the Museum of Modern Art, then, have great authority in determining what is or is not to be viewed as art. Its directors include such illustrious names as

David Rockefeller, Chairman of the board of Chase Manhattan Bank;

John Hay Whitney, centimillionaire, former publisher of the *New York Herald Tribune* and ambassador to Great Britain;

William S. Paley, Chairman of the Board of CBS;

Mrs. C. Douglas Dillon, wife of Douglas Dillon;

Mrs. Edsel B. Ford, widow of Edsel B. Ford (son of Henry Ford) and mother of Henry Ford II; and

Mrs. John D. Rockefeller III, wife of oldest of four sons of John D. Rockefeller, Jr.

The Lincoln Center for the Performing Arts in New York City is a major influence in the nation's serious theatre, ballet, and music. The Lincoln Center houses the Metropolitan Opera, the New York Philharmonic, and the Julliard School of Music. It also supports the Lincoln Repertory Company (theatre), the New York State Theatre (ballet), and the Library-Museum for Performing Arts. These component parts exercise some independence, but the Lincoln Center's board of directors has considerable formal responsibility over all of these activities. In 1979, the chairman of the board of the Lincoln Center was John D. Rockefeller III, the oldest of the Rockefeller brothers.

The Metropolitan Opera, which opened in 1883, is the nation's most influential institution in the field of serious operatic music. Decisions about what operas to produce influence greatly what is or is not to be considered serious opera in America and indeed the world. Such decisions are the formal responsibility of a board that included (as of 1979) such luminaries as

Mrs. August Belmont, a daughter of the Saltonstalls of Massachusetts;

William Rockefeller, a cousin of the Rockefeller brothers and a senior partner of Shearman and Sterling, a top Wall Street law firm;

Edward M. Kennedy, U.S. Senator from Massachusetts;

Mrs. J. W. Marriott, wife of president of Marriott Hotels, himself a heavy financial contributor to political candidates;

Jacqueline Kennedy Onassis, the former Mrs. John F. Kennedy;

Charles H. Percy, U.S. Senator from Illinois;

Elliott M. Richardson, former Secretary of Health, Education and Welfare, Secretary of Defense, and Attorney General; and

Arthur H. Schlesinger, Jr., former Special Assistant to President John F. Kennedy, member of the Trilateral Commission.

Notes

1. See *Minority Grants Report* for 1976.

2. See Grace Glueck, "Record Budget for the Arts Gain," *New York Times*, 12 May 1977, p. 26C.

3. Heading the special committee was Dr. Archie L. Buffkins of the University of Maryland, a consultant to the Kennedy Center on minority affairs. Other members of the committee included Thomas Hoving, former director of the Metropolitan Museum of Art; Quincy Jones; Billy Taylor; Katherine Dunham; Nancy Wilson; and Ellen Steward.

4. See Helen C. Smith, "How The South Gets Gypped," *Atlanta Constitution*, 1 June 1978, p. 1B.

5. *Ibid.*

6. *Ibid.*

7. *Ibid.*

8. *Ibid.*

9. *Ibid.*

10. Thomas R. Dye, *Who's Running America?: The Carter Years*, 2nd ed. (Englewood Cliffs, NJ: Prentice-Hall, Inc., 1979), p. 123.

11. *Ibid.*

Conclusion

As demonstrated by the available evidence, including the United States House of Representatives Appropriations Committee's Investigative Report, the Endowment has perpetuated programs and practices that are discriminatory. The Endowment's policies have clearly shown that it is not seriously concerned about its notion of being committed to "cultural pluralism." It continues to lack geographic, racial, as well as broad-based representation in its support of the various arts disciplines. The available evidence supports the charges that the NEA provides tremendous financial and technical support to a "centralized" culture power that exists. As a result of their positions of influence with certain political and economic institutions and organizations, a select few individuals virtually establish, dictate, and control the cultural apparatus in American society through the National Arts Endowment.

The Endowment is basically concerned with identifying, relating to, and assisting Euro-American culture. Irrespective of the arguments that it offers to the contrary, this was the practicing reality at the time that the research was conducted for this book. Although the Endowment instituted a number of changes over time, such as a rotation of personnel policy, compartmentalizing and specializing in particular parts of its program area, it has not addressed itself to any fundamental alteration of its established structure or practices. To reemphasize points that were argued by Endowment Chairman Biddle when speaking before the U.S. Senate's Committee on Labor and Human Resources, the effort is not so much to deny outright that certain groups and individuals benefit from the Endowment and others do not in equal proportion. He articulated in his presentation more of a justification than a denial, when questioned about the charges of "elitism" and "populism" and how the arts were being polarized. Biddle responded, "It seems to me that 'elitism' can indeed mean quality, can indeed mean 'the Best'—and 'populism' I would suggest can mean 'access'." In

Biddle's words, individuals should have access to the best there is in the arts. It so happens that "the best" is determined by some individuals and institutions for other individuals and other institutions. In this particular case, "the best" ends up being culture that is determined by middle- to upper-income white Euro-Americans. What this actually means is that "the best" is symphony, philharmonic, opera, and chamber-type institutions and organizations. As indicated by a study that looked at "Median Income of Audience by Art Form," the median of median incomes for orchestras and operas was $20,000 to $21,000, and the range of median income was between $18,000 and $28,000. This was several years ago, which suggests that it is much higher today. In spite of all that it has done and even that which it is proposing to do, the NEA's policies do not reflect the cultural diversity that exists in America.

The discrimination case involving the John F. Kennedy Center for the Performing Arts in Washington, D.C., is not an isolated case among the Endowment's major grantees. The Endowment's major grantees exemplify the same type of posture as does the Endowment itself. As indicative of the racial and class nature of the Endowment, in 1975 it awarded $14,216,346 to cultural institutions and organizations in Greater New York. Black institutions and organizations received only 5.2 percent of the total amount awarded. The 1976 Minority Grants Report further supported the charges that the policies and practices of the Endowment are of a race and class nature. At the 1979 hearings on the arts held in Washington, Congressional Black Caucus member Congresswoman Shirley Chisholm argued that minority applicants receive only five percent of funds allocated by the Endowment.

The Endowment also has not moved to ensure that it becomes more responsible to the public that it is designated to serve. Even a recommendation by the Justice Department and its own legal counsel that it appoint an Equal Opportunity Employee (EOE) Officer was not acted upon. Instead, the line position was eliminated altogether. The "elevation" of Gordon Braithwaite to the position of Special Assistant for Minority Concerns, even in Braithwaite's own words, had no real effect or impact on the overall program and policy activities of the Endowment. In fact, his role has even been referred to simply as one of a spectator. As evident in its funding policy and a specific charge raised by Representative Chisholm, the Endowment has tended to operate with more of an "anti-community" arts posture. In many respects, this has to do with the content and purpose of "community art,"[1] as opposed to "art for art's sake" that is perpetuated by mainstream Euro-American cultural institutions and organizations. In Congresswoman Chisholm's words, neighborhood arts are not seen as "legitimate" art.

The posture of the government today has changed only in form. During the 1930s in particular, the government was more overt in its censorship toward certain cultural expressions. Today, as the arts become more and more of a recognized tool for communication and cultural identity in American society, the government used the Endowment as the vehicle by which it dictates cultural policy for the nation. Although the Endowment does not enforce Affirmative Action or Title VI Civil Rights regulations, the government does nothing to make constructive and innovative enforcement of violations by the Endowment. A primary example of this attitude by the government was demonstrated by the fact that Justice Department, instead of enforcing the law, only recommended that the Endowment hire an Equal Opportunity Employee Officer.

In a sense, the Endowment's practices of discrimination in hiring and staffing procedures, unequal distribution of grants and technical assistance, and geographic imbalance in all of these matters are ignored by the government. Although the Endowment has begun to have some effect on altering the geographic imbalance that existed, the same cannot be said for its race and class posture. As one of its strongest critics in the Congress, Congresswoman Chisholm argued that the various changes made by the Endowment would have some impact in enhancing the diversity of the review process. However, she warned that there was a fundamental problem with such an approach: "It does not go to the core issue: who will be responsible for overseeing access and equity in the Endowment's programs?"

Notes

1. "Community arts" in this respect is used as a code meaning black cultural activities, because other forms of "community arts" are recognized as legitimate. See *Jet Magazine*, "Is there a Future for Black Talent in the Theatre?" 9 August 1979, p. 63. In an interview, Broadway producer Woody King, Jr., commented about why there is a lack of support for black cultural activities, especially theatre, from the white community. King pointed out that the theatre is an instrument by which messages can be conveyed. King talked about how many black plays tend to speak to the "ills of America," for which whites are responsible. This has a lot to do with how American society views black cultural activities.

Appendix A

Text of Congresswoman Shirley Chisholm's Testimony Before the House Appropriations Subcommittee on Interior, 8 May 1979[1]

After a meeting last October with the Arts and Humanities Braintrust, Chairman Biddle agreed to establish an Office for Minority Concerns to enhance opportunities for minority participation at the Endowment. The need for such an office was supported by evidence contained in the 1976 Minority Grants Report. During that year, at least four of the Endowment['s] twelve programs awarded no money to minorities in three categories of grants: Individual, Organizations, and Project. For example, no minority individual received grants under the Media Arts or Museum Programs. Incredibly, the Fed-state program did not fund a single minority project in 1976. The NEA has never provided the Congressional Black Caucus or anyone else for that matter with any extensive record stipulating their current awards to minority groups. The real allocation of awards to minorities is a figure that can only be guessed at.

Unfortunately, Mr. Chairman, examples of these funding equities [are] only too evident. An example of the lack of minority access to NEA funds can be seen in the small number of awards to historically Black colleges when compared with awards made to all colleges and universities. Out of $4.1 million available to post-secondary institutions, only four awards totaling $45,000 were awarded to Black colleges last year. The same access problem can be seen in the equally small number of awards to minority firms. Again, to date there have been only four minority firms who received contracts from the NEA. Last year, eight Black dance companies were denied touring funds by the NEA. Dance companies often rely heavily on touring to bring in additional revenue to maintain their home seasons. Further, the denial of funds to these companies limited their ability to present their particular unique talents to isolated areas of this country which are totally unfamiliar with these artists. In the Challenge Grant Program, of the 309 challenge grantees, only 15 have been minority organizations.

The question then becomes what impact has the Office of Minority Concerns had on these . . . statistics? While the office's director Gordon Braithwaite has had several important accomplishments during his short six-month tenure, the office in its present structure, can't possibly do the kind of comprehensive work that is needed to influence policy in all areas of the NEA. A change of policy priorities is the key to minority access at the Endowment. One of the major drawbacks to access is the lack of minorities in top-level positions at the Endowment. The latest data indicate that of the approximately 80 minorities, 44 (or 55%) of them are concentrated in clerical positions from GS-1 to GS-7. The problem here again is priorities. It is difficult to believe that the NEA is committed to increased minority participation when, out of 325 staff positions, only five minorities are at a GS-15 level. In fact, two of these five positions have no direct program authority but report directly to Chairman Biddle as Special Assistant for Minority Concerns and New Constituencies. Of the 15 senior-level positions, with program authority, only two of these are presently minorities. Without program authority, you are outside of the mainstream of Endowment activity. Consequently, it is extremely difficult to have a direct influence on policies related to accessibility. This has unfortunately become the fate of the Office of Minority Concerns.

What is even more critical to affecting change for minorities at the NEA is the total absence of minorities in any policymaking position at the Endowment. For example, the policymaking role of the Office of Minority Concerns could have been elevated if the responsibility for some of the programs that were formally administered by the Deputy Chairman for Intergovernmental Relations had been transferred to that office rather than dispersed between two deputies. This would have allowed the Office of Minority Concerns to at least enter the mainstream of Endowment activity. We should remember that in any game plan, you are likely to score more points as a participant rather than a spectator. The Office of Minority Concerns' present spectator role is not conducive to promoting major change in the Endowment's priorities.

These problems and others were fully acknowledged by the Department of Justice when it rejected the NEA's Title VI Compliance Plan in July of last year. The Federal Program Section of the Civil Rights Division found the plan unacceptable because it failed to cite the following specific matters: time tables/internal controls for reviews; allocation staff; guidelines; civil rights training; use of continuing state programs and their obligations (28 C.F.R. Section 42.210).

Nondiscrimination by Recipients of Endowment Funds

Over the many months that I have studied the operation of the Endowment, I have identified several compliance problems involving an imbalance in the distribution of federal funds to recipient state art councils, as well as individual grantees. For example, allegations have been brought to my attention which raise serious doubt about the ability of the Endowment to ensure hat federal statutory prohibitions barring discrimination based on race, color, national origin, sex, and handicapped are enforced at the state and national level. For example, charges of discrimination in the allocation of grants awarded by state art councils have resulted in referrals to the Justice Department. Without a systematic approach and administrative remedy available for the speedy resolution of complaints involving discrimination, many more individuals will be forced to experience unnecessary delays in receiving a response to their charges. My investigations leaves little doubt that bias in program and activities funded under the Endowment will persist until the agency has at its disposal a mechanism to ameliorate these problems.

Title VI Compliance

The legislative mandate of the Endowment's authorizing legislation, which establishes a grant-in-aid program to the states (Section 5(g) of the Act), requires that funds allocated directly to the states be used for the development of "projects and productions in the arts in such a manner as will furnish adequate programs; facilities and services in the arts to all the people and communities in each of the several states." Many states' arts councils have been negligent in monitoring the use of these funds on a local level, as well as making them available on an equal basis to residents of that state. Title VI Compliance requirements stipulate that the responsibility for the implementation of its provisions lies with the head of each agency extending federal financial assistance (42 U.S.C., Section 2000-1). Section 42.415 of the Civil Federal Rules require[s] that an agency's compliance plan has or intends to satisfy each specific matter of its overall Title VI responsibility. This is required even if that agency, like the NEA, may not perform certain enforcement activities due to a delegation agreement. Further, where an agency provides assistance to continuing state programs, for example state arts councils, a procedure or system designed to ensure that such recipients have established a Title VI Program for itself and its sub-recipients is mandated. Fed-state and others within the Endowment will continue or increase their contributions to local and state arts groups. Consequently, it is imperative that NEA continue to monitor state plans for equitable access.

General Policy Issues

Several policy issues have come to my attention in reviewing NEA's access problems. These issues must be addressed if the Endowment is to increase accessibility beyond the "closed circle" as discussed in your staff investigation report. Program directors must actively encourage panels to view applicants as serious candidates for funding under a given program. Currently, Expansion Arts, Folk Arts and Special Projects programs are looked to as the programs for minorities and other non-traditional arts groups. While Expansion Arts has assisted many community-based arts groups and new arts programs, it should not be seen as the "dumping ground" for any proposal with a minority component. The same principle would apply to folk arts. Rural artists have benefited tremendously from this program through workshops and festivals funded by the NEA. But these artists should not be confined exclusively to Folk Arts as their only source of Endowment monies. They should be able, for example, to apply to Visual Arts, if their talent is in the visual arts, with the same consideration they would have received as a Folk Arts' applicant.

Recommendations

I believe that the Office of Minority Concerns can never be a catalyst for real change as it is presently structured. A Special Assistant for Minority Concerns, with a secretary and contractual consultant, is hardly enough to influence access policy for twelve different programs. This position should be elevated to a deputy chair for access and equity. The person would then have specific responsibility for generating policy to enhance the under-representation of such groups as minorities, rural and community artists. The vacuum of a specific policy person in this area contributes to the low priority this issue has received to date. I recognize that this new position would require the allocation of an additional GS-16 position to the agency. The rationale was given to explain the present structure of the Office of Minority Concerns. It is obvious that the Office of Minority Concerns can't really generate any policy changes in the NEA's administrative apparatus. It is evident to me that without this position not very much will change at the Endowment. I am aware of the investigative report of this committee, which recommends a reorganization of the NEA's panel structure. Although I believe that this would enhance the diversity of the review process, I feel it does not go to the core issue: who will be responsible for overseeing access and equity in the Endowment's programs? Certainly, twelve different programs could not be expected to handle that responsibility. It is for this reason that I strongly support the creation of a third Deputy Chairman. This deputy chair position is the only way that access for minorities and others can be assured. Further, I feel that language should be attached to the FY '80 appropriation for the NEA which will require that the Endowment develop a plan for increasing access for underrepresented groups. This will force the Endowment to reassess its priorities and develop some strategies for increasing opportunities for all of America's artists.

Notes

1. Hearing Before the Subcommittee on Education, Arts, and Humanities of the Committee on Labor and Human Resources: United States Senate, 96th Congress, 1st Sess. on S. 1386, 26, 27, and 28 June 1979.

Appendix B

Growth in Selected Cultural Institutions Eligible for Funding, 1965–1978*

Types of Institutions	1965	1978
Professional Symphony Orchestra	58	144
Professional Opera Companies	27	65
Large Professional Theaters	12	70
Small Professional Theaters	10	200
Professional Dance Companies	37	200
Museums (art, science, history)	1700	1800
Media Arts Centers	1	15
Artists Spaces	0	200
State Arts Agencies (including territories and District of Columbia)	7	56

*Estimated

Appendix C

NASAA Letter

September 20, 1977

The Honorable Sidney Yates
Chairman
Subcommittee on the Interior
Committee on Appropriations
House of Representatives
Room B-308
Rayburn House Office Building
Washington, D.C. 20515

Dear Mr. Chairman:

At its Annual Meeting held in Salt Lake City, Utah, September 16-18, 1977, the National Assembly of State Arts Agencies considered the matter of funding for "small groups and struggling artists." Representatives of the National Endowment for the Arts presented their proposed guidelines for distribution of $3.6 million in grants to the above-named applicants. I have been instructed by unanimous resolution to convey the following points to you on behalf of the Assembly.

First, it is of utmost importance to declare that state arts agencies as a group and individually share the concerns for assisting small groups and struggling artists. Most, if not all of them, now serve these applicants with a wide variety of grants and services, using state-appropriated funds and Federal received from the National Endowment for the Arts. The state arts agencies have communication lines open to these applicants, have mechanisms in place to serve them and, perhaps

most important, have the perspective to make informed and fair decisions about them by virtue of experience and proximity.

There is no question in our minds that more funds are needed to
serve these applicants, among others. As you have heard in testimony
and other contacts from state arts agency leaders, we encourage and ap-
plaud your continued efforts to raise the Federal appropriations for the
arts. Having discussed the Endowment's efforts to design a program
based on Congress's stated desire to see this constituency better-served,
we respectfully submit that we have strong apprehensions that those
efforts will fail to achieve the intended goal. For this reason, we are
recommending that the Endowment immediately suspend its plans until
more effective cooperative explorations and planning can be completed
to meet this mutually held goal.

Some would characterize this position as one motivated by a desire
for greater power for the state arts agencies. We urge you to reject such
a notion and accept our recommendation on its merits, understanding
that it comes from a deep concern for serving the clientele in the most
effective way. We would also like to note that we realize and accept the
fact that our recommendation would at least temporarily suspend the
distribution of the mandated 20% of the $3.6 million to the states and/
or regions.

The substance of our apprehension is that the current plan
proposed by the Endowment would not meet the stated goal, and quite
possibly, would create unmet expectations, disappointments, frustra-
tion, and hostility among the very clients it is aimed to serve. The previously ineligible applicants who might benefit from these proposed
programs are large in number and eager for new funding sources, as are
all the arts. The creation of new mechanisms at the Endowment and the
augmentation of existing ones will have profound implications at the
Endowment itself, which already has over 150 categorical programs, an
astounding number for so small an agency. We have conflicting
feelings—a sincere recognition of and desire to meet the needs of the
proposed beneficiaries contrasted to a real fear that the Endowment will
not be able to sustain the effects of its proposed actions with a rela-
tively modest amount of funds.

For a speedy resolution and implementation of the program, we
would propose to immediately re-open the planning, this time with
meaningful participation by representatives of the intended clientele,
state arts agencies, community arts agencies, the national arts service
organizations and the Endowment. This planning should examine every
possible option to meet the proposed goal, with explanations of the

financial administrative and policy implications of each option. We would propose that you and your colleagues and/or staff either be direct participants in these explorations or that you be kept apprised of their progress and receive a report on the results. In this way, a full understanding of the subject matter would be achieved, to the satisfaction of all affected interests.

This subject, to which you gave constructive special recognition in your latest deliberations, is too consequential to be addressed in a hasty and superficial manner. We trust that you will agree that to proceed as we have recommended will greatly increase the possibility that the job will be done right.

I, and any number of my colleagues, would be happy to meet with you at your conveniences to discuss this in greater detail.

Sincerely yours,
/S/ Stephen Sell
Chairman
National Assembly of State Arts Agencies

Appendix D

Median Income of Audience By Art Form

Art Form	Median of Median Incomes* $	Range of Median Incomes $	Total # of Studies
All museums	17,158	13,394–30,618	18
Art museums	18,148	14,016–30, 618	10
History museums	16,757	13,394–29,055	3
Science museums	17,269	14,765–20,851	5
All performing arts	18,903	9,466–28,027	70
Ballet and dance	20,082	16,452–22,404	10
Theater, Excluding Outdoor drama	19,342	9,469–25,784	27
Theater, Including Outdoor drama	16,819	9,466–25,784	45
Orchestra	20,825	18,221–28,027	11
Opera	21,024	19,017–27,245	5

*In constant mid-1976 dollars.

Source: Research Division Report #9, National Endowment for the Arts, *Audience Studies of the Performing Arts and Museums, A Critical Review*, November 1978, Table 6, p. 30. A study by Paul Dimaggio, Michael Useem, and Paula Brown, Center for the Study of Public Policy, November, 1977.

On the subject of "Race and Ethnicity," the report concluded that "The relative paucity of blacks and other racial and ethnic minorities in arts audiences has been commented on frequently and, indeed, has been a matter of some concern to the arts community." In 1972, the American Association of Museums called attention to the problem of making museums relevant and hospitable to inner-city and minority people, noting that the movement of the middle class to the suburbs and of African Americans, Mexican-Americans, and Puerto Ricans to the core city "have left the museum, and urban institution, to some extent a beached whale" (See American Association of Museums, 1972, p. 6).

Bibliography

Books

Bensman, Joseph and Bernard Rosenberg. *Mass, Class and Bureaucracy*. Englewood Cliffs, NJ: Prentice-Hall, Inc., 1963.

Caute, David. *The Dancer Defects: The Struggle for Cultural Supremacy During the Cold War*. New York: Oxford University Press, 2003.

Cummings, Jr., Milton C., and Richard S. Katz (Eds.). *The Patron State: Government and the Arts in Europe, North America, and Japan*. New York: Oxford University Press, 1987.

Cummings, Jr., Milton C., and J. Mark Davidson Schuster (Eds). *Who's to Pay for the Arts?: The International Search for Models of Arts Support*. New York: American Council for the Arts Books, 1989.

de Tocqueville, Alexis. *Democracy in America*. New York: Century Co., 1898.

Dye, Thomas R. *Who's Running America?: The Carter Years*, 2nd ed. Englewood Cliffs, NJ: Prentice-Hall, Inc., 1979.

Fulbright, J. William, *The Pentagon Propaganda Machine*. New York: Liveright, 1970.

Horowitz, Irving Louis (ed.). *Power, People and Politics: The Collected Essays of C. Wright Mills*. New York: Oxford University Press, 1974.

Levine, Faye. *The Cultural Barons: An Analysis of Power and Money in the Arts*. New York: Thomas Y. Crowell Company, 1976.

Overmyer, Grace. *Government and the Arts*. New York: W. W. Norton and Company, Inc., 1939.

Newspapers

The Atlanta Constitution
The Atlanta Daily World

The Atlanta Journal
Chronicle of Higher Education
The New York Times
Washington International Arts Letter

Journals

Grassroots and Pavement (GAP), A National Journal of Neighborhood
    Arts

Magazines

Art In America
Arts News
Black Enterprise
Jet
U.S. News & World Report

Newsletters

The Cultural Post (National Endowment for the Arts)
For The People (Congressional Black Caucus)
Survival (Queens-Inner City Arts Council)

Manuals

NEA: Guide To Programs
U.S. Government Manual, 1979–1980

Reports

Minority Grants Report (1976)
NEA Annual Reports

Acts

Arts, Humanities, and Museum Services Act of 1979, Public Law 96-
496.

Index

About the Author

Jerry Henderson was born in Troy, Alabama. He is a graduate of the Troy City Public School System. He earned a Bachelor of Arts in Political Science from Brooklyn College, Brooklyn, New York, and a Master of Arts in Political Science from Atlanta University, Atlanta, Georgia.

Henderson participated as a grassroots activist organizer and strategist in the black arts community of New York City, which challenged the New York State Council on the Arts, New York City/Bureau of Cultural Affairs, and the National Endowment on the Arts. The challenges were designed to have blacks, artists, arts institutions, and organizations recognized and be included in decision making, staffing, grants, awards, and appropriations.

Since taking an active role in the arts community in New York City and Atlanta, Georgia, he has served as an elected public official, an appointed public official, an adjunct professor of political science and government, and an international consultant in the area of democracy and governance.

He is a National Award Winning writer. His articles have appeared in *Speakin' Out News, County Compass, The New York Voice, Montgomery Advertiser, Our Time Press, The Atlanta Voice, Daily Challenge, The Messenger, Elections Today, The Progress, and Frontline.* He is the author of two other books and several published reports and papers.

Henderson is a member/affiliate of several national, state, and international organizations and institutions and is a member of the Board of Directors of a national organization and an international organization.

He is the father of one daughter, Zakiya, who is a first-year college student.

Other books by Jerry Henderson

Seeking Public Political Office in the United States: A Candidate's Guide to Seeking Public Office

The Politics of Exclusion: Bizarre Court Decisions and Congressional Redistricting